Sadat
and his Statecraft

Sadat
and his Statecraft

FELIPE FERNANDEZ-ARMESTO

First published 1982
Second edition 1983

British Library Cataloguing in Publication Data.
Fernandez-Armesto, Felipe
Sadat and his Statecraft. 2nd ed.
1. Sadat, Anwar el-   2. Egypt
   Presidents Biography
   Title
962´.054´0924   DT 107.828.S23
ISBN 0-946041-14-8

Published by The Kensal Press, Shooter's Lodge, Windsor Forest, Berkshire. Printed and bound in Great Britain by Hollen Street Press Ltd, Slough

PREFACE TO THE SECOND EDITION

The first edition of this book was written and rushed through the press in the immediate aftermath of Sadat's murder. For this new edition I have modified some hasty or intemperate judgements; type-setting and editorial errors have been corrected; and it has been possible to make limited revisions to the text to take account of the scholarly work and journalistic revelations of the last twelve months. I have not revised the predictions made in the Epilogue as readers may prefer to judge for themselves which prophecies have proved true and which false: some, of course, have yet to be tested.

F.F.-A.

Oxford   29th January 1983

PREFACE TO THE FIRST EDITION

On 6th October, 1981, when President Sadat was assassinated in Cairo, the world — according to the British Prime Minister — became 'a more dangerous place'. No other life seemed more critical to global peace. It was typical of Sadat that he should dominate the world stage even in death. He was a politician capable of generating extraordinary extremes of adulation and hatred. His reputation veered in his lifetime from acclaim to opprobrium and now hangs in the balance. His ability to capture public imagination all over the world was unrivalled in his lifetime. Now that he is dead, interest in his life and work has quickened and apprehension about his legacy has increased.

That is why I have written this study. Its purpose is to explore some problems of critical importance or deep curiosity concerning Sadat: the source, nature and extent of his impact on events; the strange power he had to compel the attention of the world: the roots (in his own personality and recent history) of his work and distinctive political style. In particular, I want to try to weigh Sadat's historical standing in the immediate aftermath of his murder.

Sadat himself profoundly believed that the individual can impress the mark of his will on historical events. For him, human history was by no means the playing of vast, impersonal, uncontrollable forces but rather a genuinely human creation, yielding, under God, to moulding by individual hands. It is proper to ask how far his own career illustrates that belief. How far does he belong to that small class of world leaders who are not merely borne along by the tide of history, but seem to command it from the shore? Is it fair to see him as he wished to see himself — as an active force, where most leaders are merely creative agents?

This study also aims to fulfil an acute need among students of world affairs and interested readers in general for a short but comprehensive study of Sadat's politics and policies. In recent years Sadat and his Egypt have attracted a great deal of attention from scholars and journalists. There have been some impressive general surveys of Sadat's Egypt, such as those of J. Waterbury, *Egypt* (Bloomington and London, 1978); R. M. Burrell and A. R. Kelidar, *Egypt: the Dilemmas of a Nation, 1970-77* (Washington Papers, no. 48, Beverley Hills and London, 1977) and M. Aulas and others, *L'Égypte d'aujourd'hui* (Paris, 1977). A number of thematic studies have contributed to knowledge of the subject. Among the most notable are those of R. Mabro *(The Egyptian Economyu,* Oxford, 1974) and E. Kanovsky *(The Egyptian Economy since the Mid-sixties: the micro-sectors,* Tel Aviv, 1978) on the economy; A. Z. Rubinstein *(Red Star over the Nile,* Princeton, 1977) and F. M. Shalaby *(Der Wandel der ägyptischen Außenpolitik unter Sadat, 1970 bis 1977,* Bonn, 1979), M. Heikal *(The Road to Ramadan,* New York, 1975) on foreign policy; and I. Harik *(The Political Mobilisation of Peasants: a study of an Egyptian Community,* Bloomington, 1974) and L. Binder *(In a Moment of Enthusiasm,* Chicago, 1978) on the interface of political and social history. Authors of articles and short, selective essays have made valuable contributions, too many to enumerate in full, though a few important examples may be mentioned, such as B. Witte, 'Fünf Jahre Sadat', *Europa-Archiv,* xxx (1975); E. N. Slaieh, 'The October War and Sadat's Year of Decision', *International Political Science Review,* x, no. 2 (1975); J. Waterbury, 'Egypt: the Wages of Dependency', in A. L. Udovitch, ed., *The Middle East: Oil, Conflict and Hope* (Lexington, 1976); D. M. Reid, 'Return of the Egyptian Wafd', *International Journal of African Historical Studies,* xii (1979); N. Salem-Babikian, 'The Sacred and the Profane; Sadat's Speech to the Knesset,' *Middle East Journal,* xxxiv (1980). In addition there has been a striking political essay by R. W. Baker (*Egypt's Uncertain Revolution under Nasser and Sadat*, Cambridge, Mass., 1978) which has posed some central problems for students of Sadat's work. R. Israeli has added significantly to the useful literature by gathering a great mass of documentation together in *The Public Diary of President Sadat* (3 vols.; Leyden, (1978). The Algiers *Revue de Presse*, the *Arab Report* of London and the *Middle East Economic Digest* have kept the world abreast of events in Egypt. Meanwhile, the only full-length biographical studies of Sadat have been an extraordinarily tedious and repetitive work by B. Narayan *(Anwar El-Sadat, Man with a Vision,* New Delhi, 1977) and Sadat's brilliant and exciting autobiography, *In Search of Identity* (New York, 1977), a book which is a splendid mine of source material and of insights into the workings of Sadat's mind and heart; but the autobiography is written as a literary experiment and philosophical exploration as much as a contribution to the historical record. It presents a kaleidoscopic vision of the elements of Sadat's life and policies — dazzling, variegated, forming and re-forming into sudden, random, evanescent patterns — which the present work aims to sort out, analyse, clarify.

Despite all these contributions, no general assessment of Sadat's achievement has so far been set before the public. There is only scope at present, of course, for an interim assessment. Sadat's story has still to be unfolded and the hidden leaves may yet change its overall appearance. It will be many years before crucial official documents and personal papers are revealed. Only a rough-hewn image of Sadat can be presented here. Nevertheless, there are some aspects of his life and work which are of urgent public interest. There are clear themes in his policies which can already be identified and discussed. In the course of his career Sadat created a distinctive statecraft. Analysis of it should help readers not only to understand Egypt's recent past but also to assess her likely future course under the President's posthumous influence. Finally, the character, inspiration and ideals which underlay his actions can be studied well enough now, with advantages for our comprehension of the mainsprings of Sadat's response to problems which still face his successor and — in some measure — many other world leaders. This book, in short, is an attempt at an interim assessment of Sadat's achievement, an anatomy of his statecraft, and a search for an explanation of the spiritual and intellectual sources of his approach to politics.

It is too much to hope to be objective about a subject of contemporary history. The present work was begun in a spirit of critical detachment but has become, in part, a valedictory tribute. Sadat has enthralled me, as he enthralled millions — especially, like a prophet without honour, in countries other than his own. His startlingly original contributions to politics command respect and demand acknowledgement. He made mistakes. He was driven to extemporisation, though rarely to expediency. He failed from time to time in the struggle to uphold his own intentions and ideals and left them unfulfilled at his end. Personal and political decline afflicted him in his last year of life. It would be a savage injustice to him — as one of the more honest and self-critical of statesmen — to overlook or suppress the facts that modify his renown. But at the end of the day, even the most dispassionate observer finds some degree of esteem irresistible. Those who come to criticise go away to praise. When adverse judgements have been made, especially on the errors and inconsistencies of the last months of his régime, admiration remains for the greatness of many aspects of his vision of peace and prosperity for the Middle East, which the present writer, for one, hopes will long survive him.

F.F.-A.

Shooter's Lodge,
Windsor Forest,
Berkshire

November 1981

Note on Additions

Some passages have been added to the Epilogue between completion of the book and final printing.

Note on References

References in the text are indicated by author, date and page number only. Full references can be identified from the list of selected further reading in European languages, which will be found at the end of the book (page 180). References to articles in newspapers are by title and date.

F.F.-A

February 1982

Contents

In the Name of God, Most Gracious, Most Merciful

God is the Light
Of the heavens and the earth.

The parable of His light
Is as if there were a Niche
And within it a Lamp;

The Lamp enclosed in Glass:
The Glass as it were
A brilliant Star:
Lit from a blessed Tree,

An Olive, neither of the East
Nor of the West,
Whose oil is wellnigh
Luminous,
Though fire scarce touched it:

Light upon light!
God doth guide
Whom He will
To His Light:

God doth set forth parables
For Men: and God
Doth know all things.

— Surat al-nur

CHAPTER ONE

The Setting and the Background

When Father Ayrout asked the children of his mission school to add the missing features to the outlines of a house sketched on the blackboard, they were told to draw windows, stairs, doors and 'neighbours' (giran) [Mabro, 1974, 43]. This was the Egypt in which Anwar El-Sadat was born and brought up: the Egypt of countless small, intimate village communities, crammed into the tight, lush space of the Nile valley — so closely and in circumstances so demanding of mutual communal help that life without neighbours would be unthinkable. In the same Egypt the vast majority of Egyptians have spent their lives and labours for centuries under conditions which have barely altered in essentials, because the geographical factors are so clear-cut and their determinism so inescapable.

There are only about eight-and-a-half million cultivable *feddans* in Egypt. The other ninety-six per cent of the soil is almost unyielding, almost implacable desert. Only in recent years has the cultivable figure been so high: some fifty years ago, only six million *feddans* were tilled — and the rate of increase of population since then has been more than double that of the increase in tillage. Down a narrow, shallow valley, where over thirty million people jostle and join and struggle for survival, the Nile runs like an unhealed gash, bleeding gently, rhythmically, regularly; for its periodic inundations are lifeblood indeed to the Egyptians gathered, half-grateful, half-apprehensive, on its banks. Through Upper Egypt it grinds rather than runs. Its pace is generally slow below Aswan and is sustained only by the weight of its own waters. No tributary flows to meet it. The climate is hot and dry, with hardly a drop of corrupting moisture in the air: thus the immortality the pharaohs craved has been accorded to their monuments. In Lower Egypt, the long arm of the river — its muscles all concentrated in the distant cataracts — seems to stretch feeble finger-tips to the sea, as if making a last effort after exhausting exertions. Here, in the delta, the air is humid and oppressive, the soil marshy and unhealthy.

Egypt has had pharaohs and caliphs, dynasts and despots, satraps and sultans, but the real dictator has always been the river. Like all monarchs, the Nile has her mystique, the mysteries of her numinous provenance (untraced until the last century) and of her grand, goddess-like annual menstruation. Ruthless but equitable, she has forced uniform features of a pattern of life on her subjects, the Egyptian people. When they hear the seasonal chant of the local crier announcing the completion of the flood, they know how little time they have to irrigate their lands before the waters subside. The Nile is a fair tyrant: her decrees are harsh, but not capricious. Like that of many tyrants, her rule inflicts suffering but it also offers security. The alluvial deposits distributed by the flood waters create the earth which is the peasants' resource. A goddess's gift, of course, is never painlessly bestowed. Since the spread of perennial irrigation in the last century, the nitrogen content of the soil has had to be enhanced with fertilisers. Irrigation channels and drainage ducts have to be dug. Every drop of water has to be cherished against evaporation, every grain of silt guarded against waste. And the Nile is the only source of water; there are no other rivers; rainfall, except around Alexandria on the very shore of the sea, is negligible. So intensive is the labour demanded in the season that only fairly large communities, working together, can survive. Thus the Nile imposes patterns both of labour and settlement on the peasants, whose villages are spattered like a trace of shots along the river's banks — large settlements, by Middle Eastern standards, never of few than 300 inhabitants, rising to 40,000; they are jammed with dwellings not only because of the general scarcity of land and overall density of population but also because villagers prefer in-filling within the precincts of their built-up areas to sacrificing precious patches of tilled soil to housing: the greenery reaches to the very door-steps of the outermost houses of each group. [Harik, 1974,9].

The peasants form half the population; even in very recent times, they were the vast majority — two-thirds before the revolution of July 1952. For a man like Sadat, in his conception of the country and from the experience of his boyhood among peasants, they *are* Egypt; their virtues and values are Egypt's and Egyptian society as a whole, Sadat used to say, must model its institutions on peasant society. Yet the *fellahin* have no strong tradition of political action, certainly not on a national scale. Or rather, the tradition which still persisted at a regional or local level in the early nineteenth century, among bands of brigands or leagues of rival villagers, was extinguished by the agricultural revolution that Egypt's selectively enlightened despot, Mehmet Ali, then began. The brigands became commissioned policemen; village fortifications were dismantled; leagues, if not reconciled, were at least repressed. Two authoritarian régimes — those of the Albanian dynasty, founded by Mehmet Ali, and the British invaders, superimposed one on the other — effectively denied the peasantry recourse to violence against social abuses. Instead, the rustics turned to religion: devotional confraternities replaced the leagues; a quiet, resigned pietism succeeded the swelling anger and bloodlust. Only very infrequent outbursts of Mahdism could deflect peasant millenarianism back into bloodshed. The onset of quiescence had not been brought about by police action alone. The patterns of rural life had changed. Under the Mamelukes, not only were the agencies of repression rudimentary, but the state was also relatively undemanding of peasants' time and toil; the countryside fed only its own needs, with a little to spare for clergy and tax-gatherers. Irrigation — the great focus of labour — was strictly a seasonal occupation. Between times, the peasants could spend their energies as violently as they wished. Under Mehmet Ali and his successors, all that changed. Egypt was turned into a major exporter of cotton and sugar cane. The revolution in the agronomy required a revolution in methods of cultivation. Irrigation became a continuous task. Fertilisation of the soil — which the Nile's rich silts had previously accomplished unaided — became another exacting duty for the overburdened peasants. The incentive to revolt remained and was redoubled; the opportunity vanished.

Some of the peasants were armed by Mehmet Ali in his efforts to create a modern army; some participated in Mahdist risings like that at Beheira against the French; many took part in the nationalist upsurge of 1919; but on the whole, for generations before the revolution of 1952, they accepted with resignation a terrible burden of exploitation, when they were dependent on landlords for land, moneylenders for credit, and merchants for a return on their crops. Above these immediate levels of oppression perched a supreme government that was always foreign and generally imperialist, a bureaucracy that was at best indifferent and often harsh. Most estates were small, but even modest landowners had purses of indecent corpulence. While their tenants dwelt in hovels, a family of gentry like the 'Nawwar' at 'al-Barnugi' could build the splendid palace that was later occupied by the local socialist institute — modelled on one of the sumptuous khedival residences [Harik, 1974,6,48]. For most of the nineteenth century, the peasantry was abandoned to the debilitating or destructive disease of bilharzia or ankylostomiasis. Parasites bored and burrowed into their flesh, as voracious as those that lived off their labour. Faced with formidable natural foes, the peasantry were incapable of taking on political enemies. Despite a nominal law of compulsory universal education in 1933, the overwhelming majority of Egyptians and almost all the peasants were illiterate until the school-building drive of the 1950s. There could be no prospect of a revolution of the masses in early twentieth-century Egypt, like those of Mexico or China. Egypt would have to be transformed by a revolution of intellectuals.

The army, the clergy, the educational institutions, and the professions all presented backgrounds from which an intellectual revolutionary élite might emerge, but in all of them insurrection was slow to mature. The armed forces, which ultimately produced the men who made the revolution, showed some early promise: the National Party programme of 1879 had 93 officers among its 327 signatories. A group of officers, similar in their backgrounds and aspirations to the later Free Officers, essayed the first nationalist rebellion in modern Egyptian history in 1882. Their leader, Ahmad Urabi, was, like Sadat, an officer sprung from the fellahin. His pronunciamiento might have succeeded but for British intervention.

For the rest of the century the army was politically inert, cowed by the British hegemony, hamstrung by foreign sirdars; as the effects of Mehmet Ali's militarisation of the peasantry wore off, the social range of the officer class narrowed to exclude the fellahin and would not be reopened until 1936. The British also saw to it that the army was kept numerically weak — always under 15,000 in peacetime until the expansion of 1936. Secular educational institutions showed even less potential as a source of change until the foundation of a national university in 1942. Before that there was a great deal of student activism, but no framework in which it could be systematically developed. The clergy, despite their command of important channels of communication and institutions of education, were on the defensive in the late nineteenth and early twentieth centuries, when British occupation and the spread of western-inspired liberalism and scepticism undermined their position. By the end of the 1920s the qadis and shaikhs had been brought under state control; Egypt had a civil code elaborated with only the flimsiest reference to the *Sharia* or Islamic law, and an atmosphere had developed in which even prominent members of the Islamic hierarchy like Ali abdel Raqiz and Taha Husayn were advocating, in effect, the disestablishment of Islam. The rise and spread of the *Ikhwan*, the Muslim Brotherhood, in the 'thirties and 'forties symbolised a revival of militant 'Mohammedanism' in the wake of British and more generally western failures, but the Brethren did not become a serious or really promising focus of revolutionary forces until the Second World War. Finally, the professional class failed to develop any sort of revolutionary ethos until after the revolution had been carried out by others. There was fierce nationalism, especially among lawyers and teachers in the first half of this century, but no real drive for social change. Writers, who may be regarded as the mouthpiece of the professional classes, generally achieved, before the Second World War, only an emasculated nationalism that fawned on the apparently superior western world and advocated imitation as Egypt's only hope of progress — the pre-war writings of Salama Musa or Mahmud Azmi are typical. The very richness of Egypt's intellectual resources, the strength of her educational traditions and institutions, and the people's resentment — diffused through all classes — of their national humiliation at Britain's hands, all these features of Egyptian life in the early part of this century suggested that a degree, at least, of revolutionary potential existed. But the impetus that only determined leadership might provide was lacking. As Lenin points out in *The State and Revolution,* a revolution needs leaders: the forces of history cannot generate revolution without the aid of tightly knit, highly motivated vanguards.

The classes outside the peasantry and intelligentsia were of little social or political importance before the uprising of 1952. Just as the peasants were crushed into the confines of the Nile Valley, so the townsfolk were overwhelmingly concentrated in three conurbations and a very few middle-sized towns. There was no distinct urban interest in politics, except in Cairo, which played in the Egypt of 1952 the same sort of leading, dominating role, ahead of the provinces, that Paris played in the France of 1789. Elsewhere, townsmen's mutual proximity bred no solidarity. Cairo before the revolution, though less industrialised than today, was a fully fledged megalopolis, its sprawling, chaotic personality already fully formed. The symbiosis was complete, which makes it distinctive, between a modern city laid out in the rational French manner and a higgledy-piggledy, unplanned oriental *medina*. It had a million and a half inhabitants, among whom foreigners and Copts were disproportionately well represented, introducing emulous and perhaps dangerous divisions into the city's otherwise amorphous mass. Most Cairenes engaged in crafts or commerce. There was an artisanate but hardly a proletariat, save for a tiny minority employed in the few cotton and paper mills or the sugar refinery. Other local industrial products — saltpetre, gunpowder, leather work — were produced in workshops rather than factories. In the 'forties huge numbers of students reinforced the *sans-culottes:* here was the human material that rose in street demonstrations of frightening ferocity in 1952. Alexandria, the second city, was even more a commercial emporium and international entrepôt: of its nearly three quarters of a million inhabitants, foreigners comprised a sixth. The port and the summer season — when the government migrated there to escape the mephitic Cairene heat — were its life. Port Said, as gateway to the Suez Canal, was the third town of metropolitan pretensions, with some 125,000 people. Along the coast or on the canal were a dozen other towns of more than 25,000 inhabitants, largely dependent on commerce or cotton. In the rest of Lower Egypt, only six towns exceeded 25,000 inhabitants and only one — Mahalla Kubra — had more than one large factory. A dozen more towns of the same minimum size could be found on the Upper Nile, with an occasional sugar refinery or woollens factory to dignify them. In the desert, only the oasis of Madinat-al-Fayum brought a great concentration of people together, with some 65,000 inhabitants.

The paucity of urban life and the lack of any potentially revolutionary centre outside Cairo were a consequence of industrial underdevelopment. It is, of course, a moot point whether early industrialisation would have been good for Egypt. In the early 'thirties, powerful thinkers like Mirit Butros Ghali could be found to oppose it in favour of concentration on agriculture. The fact is, however, that it happened slowly and only assumed proportions of major significance economically and industrially after the July Revolution. In 1952, industry accounted for only ten per cent of Egypt's G.N.P.; the sector's balance of payments was adverse. It employed little more than ten per cent of the labour force, most of which was tied to the manufacture of textiles and food processing, especially sugar refining which had been built up by French businessmen. Soap and cigarettes were the only other manufactures that employed large concentrations of labour. As for the mineral extraction sector, which has become so vital to Egypt today, and on which so much of her hope for the future rests, this was ridiculously callow before the revolution. Iron ore was first smelted only in 1949. Oil production had barely begun. The surface of the desert had not even been scratched.

Trade unionism was a mature growth only in a few fields: tobacco, printing and transport workers had a tradition of organised action going back to 1899 and formed their first unions by the end of the first decade of the new century, but their activities, hampered by the hostility of successive governments, were never strong enough to influence social or industrial legislation.

Almost as soon as the Second World War was over and martial law relaxed, such large groups of workers as existed began to dabble in political strikes: sugar and cotton workers in Mahalla Kubra and Cairo in 1946, for example, transport workers and petrol distributors in 1948, and almost every class of worker in the *annus mirabilis* of 1952. But these were more significant as portents of future than as statements of actual proletarian strength.

In such a setting, it is not suprising that political life was a privilege, shared, beneath democratic forms, among a factional cartel. There were political parties, which reproduced fissiparously, like amoebae, splitting one from another in petty schisms. These had little to do with matters of principle, more with ties of patronage and kin, like the interest groups that passed for parties in eighteenth-century England. They resembled commercial concerns competing for the fruits of office, rather than healthy political organisms. This situation had arisen at the end of the First World War. As the British slowly transformed Egypt from an imperial protectorate to an independent constitutional monarchy, and experiments in the party system began, a single party, the Wafd, created at the close of the war by the brilliant but mercurial Saad Zaghlul, contrived virtually to monopolise national feeling and public allegiance in Egypt. This was partly as a result of a temporary vacuum in popular politics, which the Wafd was formed just in time to fill; in part, too, it was an effect contrived by Zaghlul's genius for opportunism and propaganda. In the first post-war election under the new system in 1924, the Wafd won 195 seats out of 214. The only other parties were the Nationalists, who, despite the reputation of their founder, Mustapha Kamil, had lost credibility, and a faction of king's friends who had never possessed it.

It is worth comparing the Wafd's displacement of the Nationalist Party with the displacement in British politics of the Liberal Party by Labour, which happened at about the same time. The Nationalists were like the Liberals, and Mustapha Kamil was their Gladstone. They, too, felt obliged to nurture and coddle the newcomers, as a matter of principle, despite the long-term threat to the party's electoral viability. They found themselves overtrumped by a party that could exceed the appeal of their policies and possessed more channels of communication, more organising ability with the masses. Many of them perceived the drift of the wind, and joined the new force: in doing so, they contributed to its opportunistic character.

Three flaws vitiated the Wafd: it had to compromise its principles to take power, for the essence of the Wafd's platform was its rejection of the terms of the constitution; it was incapable of working with the king, the British or other parties, at least while Saad Zaghlul remained at its head, and in practice for most of the time even after his departure; finally, lacking any parliamentary opposition, it tended from the first to divide within itself. The party was left without a coherent policy, doomed to pursue power for its own sake and on achieving it to exploit it rather than use it for constructive purposes. Other major parties like the Ittihadists and the Saadists tended to be offshoots of the Wafd and to share its worst characteristics. The Wafd did perform one great service for Egypt's future as a democractic nation: it created a mass organisation that mobilised the political resources of ordinary people, in the towns and countryside alike; the

demonstrations it helped to organise, especially in 1919, were genuinely mass demonstrations. The pre-revolutionary political system
was not truly democratic but it did help prepare Egypt for democracy.

Mustapha Nahas Pasha, who was prime minister for the ten years
preceding the revolution, personified the deficiencies of the parties in
general and the Wafd in particular. Originally he was of the Nationalist Party, until lured to the Wafd by the patronage of Zaghlul, whom
he succeeded as leader in 1927. After brief and ineffective spells in
office in 1928 and 1930, when he displayed a gift for compromise
unimpeded by any firmness of principles, he returned to power in 1936
with some prospect of longer-term success. He negotiated the Treaty
with Britain of 1936, by which Britain's role in Egypt was more
narrowly circumscribed than previously and the degree of Egypt's
independence enhanced. This modified triumph, he hoped, would
ensure a long tenure of the premiership. He ruled like a Mameluke,
treating the state as his patrimony, filling offices of profit with place-
men and relatives, never expecting to be called to account. But he was
out-manœuvred by King Farouk, who desired a more pliable minister,
and ousted at the end of 1937. After that, he considered no recourse
too dishonourable in the effort to recover the fruits of power.
Ironically, it was the re-assertion of control by the Wafd's old foes,
the British, which accompanied the Second World War, that gave
Nahas his chance. By exploiting the Wafd's mass organisation to
foment disorder, he pressurised the British into believing that only a
Wafd government could control the country and guarantee the
stability that was vital to Britain's wartime interests. The *soi-disant*
patriot was restored to power by a British coup. On 4th February,
1942, the British ambassador informed the king, "Unless I hear by 6
p.m. that Nahas Pasha has been asked to form a cabinet, His Majesty
King Farouk must accept the consequences." That evening, British
tanks and troops surrounded the royal palace; the ambassador called on
the king with a detachment of armed men, and by nightfall Nahas was
again prime minister. The hypocrisy and greed with which the Wafd
gobbled up this milksop from the national enemy dispelled such
credibility with the people as the party still retained after the wheeler-
dealing of recent years.

The important political initiatives of the 'thirties and 'forties
came from outside the meaningless, moribund factionalism of party

and parliamentary politics. The most conspicuous sign of this was the change that overtook the Muslim Brotherhood, which had been formed to combat secularism and westernisation by awakening the Islamic inner man within every Egyptian Muslim, with a programme of individual devotional and moral regeneration. But its founder and Supreme Guide, Hassan al-Banna, was a man of political proclivities and the mood of the 'thirties was increasingly active and militant. By the end of the decade the Ikhwan was a clandestine revolutionary movement; within a few years more it had become a terrorist army. Another sign of the militant climate was the formation and fortune of *Misr al-fatat,* the Young Egypt organisation, a paramilitary camorra of student 'Green Shirts' who sought to ape the successes scored in Europe against the western liberal tradition by Fascism and Nazism. At the same time they wanted to give their movement distinctively Islamic and Egyptian tints, advocating, for instance, a return to the Sharia, the religious law, as the basis of the secular code, extolling the continuity of Egyptian history from pharaonic times and changing their name in 1940 to 'National Islamic Party'. But, as we shall see in the next chapter, the initiative which proved to be the most remarkable of the period was also the most secretive and therefore the least remarked at the time — the formation by Sadat and a few friends of a nationalist political movement among the officers of the armed forces.

Sadat's intellectual and political formation took place in the 1920s and 1930s against this background of social stagnation and injustice, economic torpor and political decadence. But he drew ideas from the study of Egypt's geography and history as well as from his perceptions of the Egypt of his day. To understand fully the setting in which the beginnings of his statecraft took shape, we have to take into account the remoter past which the young Sadat studied and the timeless geographical realities which impressed him.

The epoch of Egyptian history that meant most to young Egyptians in the 'thirties was the last age of real Egyptian independence and greatness, that is, the Pharaonic New Empire and the glorious eighteenth Dynasty. In the sixteenth century B.C. the Egyptian kingdom was conquered by the obscure Hyksos from Syria, whose overthrow by native resistance, after a hegemony of perhaps about two generations' span, marked a renaissance of Egyptian culture and a resurgence of Egyptian energy. The war was carried into the Hyksos heartlands by Thutmosis I and Thutmosis III, while the pharaohs' frontier also expanded to the south. The Pharaoh Ikhnaton, who, by imposing a species of monotheism, anticipated religious tastes his countrymen came to show centuries later, belonged to the same dynasty. Its splendours were made vividly apparent by the discovery of Tutankamun's tomb in 1922. This was a source of part of the inspiration for the new vogue for Egyptian styles in art, architecture and fashion, unequalled since the French had popularised ancient Egyptian taste in the early nineteenth century; Young Egypt, for instance, called for Cairo to be rebuilt in the ancient manner, rather as the Ptolemies had tried to copy the grandeur of the Ramesids.

The pharaohs of the eighteenth dynasty gave the New Empire a solidity that lasted half a millennium. Later, however, native rule was again interrupted by the imposition of foreign dynasties — Libyan in the tenth century B.C. and Ethiopian in the seventh. With the Persian conquest in the sixth century, the rule of genuinely native lines and kings ended, save for an interval of sixty years in the following century. Since that time, Egypt was never again under genuinely Egyptian rule. This long history of foreign tyranny made Sadat and his contemporaries look back to pharaonic times with even greater fervour, as a period of national integrity as well as national achievement. It did not seem a coincidence that autonomy and achievement should go hand in hand. From the relatively bleak period of Egyptian history between the pharaohs and their own day, young men's heroes tended to be characters of Arab or Islamic significance; of Egyptian rulers proper, only Saladin passed muster, and he of course was neither Egyptian by birth nor limited to merely Egyptian significance. But heroes are always needed in Egypt: no land has a greater density of saints and shrines and martyrs. No people is more inclined to remember its history in epic form or to recount it in terms of personalities. It was natural that men should turn to the recently canonised heroes of nationalist struggle against the British — Ahmad Urabi, who led the army revolt of 1882 and spent 20 years in exile; Mustapha Kamil, who founded the Nationalist Party and pursued the chimera of total independence with absolute intransigence, absolute ardour and absolute failure until his death in exile in 1908; and even — so inclusive was the Egyptian passion for heroes — the relatively colour-less Muhammad Farid, who succeeded Kamil as Nationalist Party head but showed little of his mentor's flair. The Nationalist Party rapidly waned — it contributed virtually nothing to the development of Egyptian politics after 1914, but the history of the nationalist move-ment as a whole absorbed the young Sadat when he was at school. To him — and here he was a representative figure of his day — the struggle against the British seemed the dominant theme of modern Egyptian history; the re-enactment of ancient glory was the consum-mation devoutly to be wished.

If ancient Egypt seemed particularly relevant to the Egypt of Sadat's youth there were aspects of the country's geography that were always equally relevant in any period. Egypt's position at the interface of three continents has not only exposed her to a wide variety of influences and made her a vector of cultural cross-fertilisation: it also gives events in Egypt peculiarly wide significance. The way she links the vital historic arteries of western and eastern civilisation — the Mediterranean and the Red Sea — gave her enormous cultural and strategic importance long before the Suez Canal. Egypt's openness to the imprint of what was best in neighbouring cultures was already apparent in pharaonic times, when Asiatic — especially Babylonian, — Cretan and Libyan influences were all absorbed and adapted. Sadat's was not the first *infitah*. If, in the course of Egyptian history as a whole, the balance of the influences has been predominantly from any one direction, it is hard to detect and perhaps does not matter much anyway.

To most Egyptians, the Arab conquest and the reception of Islam have made the biggest contribution to their culture. Sadat would not by any means have demurred at such a judgement but Europeans in Egypt can experience almost as much fellow feeling as Arabs or Muslims. Egypt is so close to Europe and has shared so many common European experiences. She was an important part of the Hellenistic and Roman worlds, and a pioneering province of Christian devotion, monasticism and evangelism. Egypt and Europe experienced a bifurcation in the seventh century A.D., but a thousand years later they began to pick up the threads again like old friends after a long separation. Egypt was the only non-European country to experience the effects of conquest by French revolutionary armies. In all the

Orient, only Japan responded more eagerly to nineteenth-century European ideas. Sadat showed throughout his career an awareness that Egypt is heir to more than one legacy; her nature consists in breadth of participation in a unique combination of civilisations.

The allure Egypt holds — because of her natural wealth or strategic position — for covetous foreign imperialisms is another ancient theme. The Russians with whom Sadat had to contend were preceded by the British and French, the latter by Turks, Crusaders, Romans and Greeks. For centuries, the saints with whose stories Egyptian devotion densely bristles, whose shrines thickly strew the middle Nile, fought spiritual wars to rid the land of demons in a strange masque of the real liberation struggle against other more substantial imperialists. Yet earlier still, in pharaonic times, the Egyptians had a long history of tenacious resistance to foreign invasion — the Thutmosids against the Hyksos, Rameses II against the Libyans, Pharaoh Necho against the Assyrians, and Amnertais of Sais against the Persians, all achieved triumphs of defence of national independence. Their example was before Sadat's eyes from his boyhood.

Sadat's response to these influences was typical of his generation. He showed no revolutionary precocity, no early gifts of leadership. He was not obviously the messianic hero for whom intellectuals like Tawfik al-Hakim were already clamouring in the 'thirties to resurrect Egypt from her prostration. He was not a particularly sensitive child. His infancy — unlike, say, Nasser's, whose drive and restlessness were honed by early misery — was conventionally happy. He rose by accident, not by any manifest destiny. He almost missed the revolution, when at last it came. He occupied a position in its inner councils lower than many potential rivals. He survived by stealth and came to supreme power late and unexpectedly, partly by his predecessor's favour, partly by others' indifference to his candidacy. He only blossomed into a charismatic leader when Nasser's mantle fell upon him and the inescapable adulation of Egyptians for their *Rais* carried him away. If he had not become president, his youth would be interesting as a thoroughly representative example of the background from which rank-and-file revolutionaries emerged in their thousands in the Egypt of the 'thirties and 'forties and early 'fifties.

This revolutionary mass grew slowly at first, really beginning to approach the critical threshold at which the revolution of 1952 became possible during the Second World War, when the numbers of the student body greatly increased and the opportunities multiplied for success in subversion and opposition. But an important stage was reached in 1936, when the size of the army and therefore of the officer corps was increased. This gave access to positions of potential influence to the first wave of young revolutionaries who had imbibed the intoxicating brew of nationalism, fascism, Marxism, scientific modernism and militant Islam that filled the loving-cups of their secret confraternities. Combined with a diet of half-baked ideologies, this had an unsettling effect on the stomach and the head. The young idealists of the revolutionary generation were united by no clear, single bond of ideology. But they did share experiences of the humiliating, abject state of their country at the time and above all they shared enemies or scapegoats in the British and the political establishment.

Their confusion probably helped them transcend their differences; for some, like Sadat in his youth, were reverential of tradition, favouring Islam and the monarchy; others, like Nasser, were devoted to technocracy and wanted to smash the old society with a steam-hammer. Others, like Khalid Muhiaddin, were, or tried to be, Marxists. But all were in reaction against the colonialism and insipid liberalism that dominated the *ancien régime.* All of those who came together in the army and air force from 1937 to 1948 were of much the same age; most were from peasant or petit-bourgeois back-grounds. They came together through the Military Academy, or garrison life, or active service or, in some cases, directly through intro-duction to revolutionary cells or terrorist groups. As one of the most representative of them, it was natural that Sadat should play an important part in bringing some of them together. The way to under-standing the revolution, and therefore the milieu in which Sadat's politics were fashioned, lies through an examination of his early life.

CHAPTER TWO

Years of Endurance

The suffering that helped to form his character came later. The first
seven years of Sadat's life were happy ones, spent in the little world of
Mit Abul Kum, the village of Upper Egypt in which he was born on
December 25th, 1918. It was a typical village and in many ways a
typical life: quiet, sequestered, regulated by the timeless rhythms of
the peasants' lot, the regular demands of the thirsty soil, the statutory
two-week irrigation period out of which each year of life was eked.
Because the young Anwar's father was generally away from home,
working in the Sudan for the British administration, it was to his
mother and grandmother that he felt closest as a child: his mother,
loving and love-inspiring; his grandmother, practical and resourceful,
a village wise-woman prescribing folk remedies for her peers, mixing
with curdled milk the warming, comforting treacle, the taste and
smell of which Sadat later recalled with vividness and pleasure [Sadat,
1978, 3, 86]. The two women taught him his first political lessons —
anti-British villagers' tales. The village was the first polity he knew,
the 'country' on which he lavished his first patriotism [Sadat, 1978, 11];
amid its friendliness and neighbourliness he felt he belonged, and the
model of the village community remained his ideal of political organisation. Years later, when he was imprisoned by the British, the
memory of his village comforted him in the Aliens' Gaol [Sadat, 1978,
42]. When he became president of his country, he urged — as we shall
see — 'the values of the village' on his fellow citizens and helped to
make peasant virtues part of the Egyptian national character.

Schooling in the village was in the hands of Shaikh Abdul Hamid
Issa, who taught Anwar the Holy Quran and the elementary general
curriculum prescribed for Quranic schools. He was a fair but exacting
master, a strict disciplinarian who demanded and got a high standard
from his pupils. He found Anwar a composed and obedient child
whose keenness showed in his preference for the front row of the class-
room. Even as a boy — for most boys are pagans — Anwar was

devout, awestruck with the idea of God the Creator. To continue his education, once the basis of Islamic learning had been imbibed, he had to go to a Coptic school near by in Tukh Delka, where his primary schooling was completed. In the visitors' book, he has since recorded his touching affection for this *alma mater,* which 'trained me and brought me up and inspired a spirit of struggle'.

In adult life, he saw school as a place of worship, for learning seemed a holy occupation and knowledge a source of sanctity. Sadat's father, who had striven to acquire enough education himself to obtain a post in the Sudan government service and was respected in the village as a learned man because he possessed a school certificate, was a great enthusiast for and believer in the virtues of education. But only one of his sons would be able to go to secondary school, and Anwar was fortunate that, for no particular reason other than his elder brother's fecklessness, the lot fell upon him. In 1925 the young Sadat went to Cairo, getting his first glimpse of broader horizons than those of the village; in 1931, at the age of twelve, he joined the Fuad I Secondary School at Abbasia. He did not have to leave his family, for his father had now returned from Sudan and set up home in Kubri al Kubbah. At the King Fuad school, it was a struggle for him to obtain his general certificate. His whole attention was already absorbed by the nationalist movement, as Sayid Ahmad Shafiq Hasb, who was a classmate and subsequently went on to the Military Academy with Sadat, has reported. While Sadat's village patriotism broadened into what he has called 'the generalised concept of a homeland' [Sadat, 1978, 11], the formal curriculum seemed restrictive, but at least there was an opportunity to read plenty of history, geography, and political science. The young Sadat got his formal qualifications, albeit with difficulty, and managed to educate himself in the process. Failures in public examinations were character-forming, for he treated them as challenges and each time went off to master the curriculum himself in time to re-sit the tests and pass.

Like most nationalists of his generation, he wanted to join the army, since — controlled though it was by the British — this was both the symbol and the hope of Egyptian independence. Until 1936 it was impossible for a man of the fellahin, without status, without wealth, without influence, to procure a place at the Military Academy, but the treaty concluded in that year provided, with British approval, for an expansion of the army. The recruitment net for officers was therefore widened. Even so, it was easier for a rich man to pass through the eye of a needle than for a poor man to enter the Royal Military Academy. Sadat was rejected by the Admissions Board, and it was only at the third attempt, by prevailing on friends to obtain an interview with Ibrahim Khayri Pasha, the chairman of the board, and gaining the invaluable help of his father's English superior officer, that the would-be cadet was given his chance. The pasha was impressed by his bearing and purposefulness. While detesting his haughtiness and condescension and all he stood for, Sadat could still feel grateful to him. He could do him a good turn later, when their power roles were reversed and Khayri came as a suppliant to Sadat. The new cadet sensed a similar delicious irony in the treaty that had helped him realise his ambition: 'the British helped me to join the Military Academy when the reason I wanted to join in the first place was to kick them out of Egypt.' [Sadat, 1978, 15].

The academy was a veritable seed-bed of revolution. The class of 1938, in which Sadat graduated, was particularly rich in revolutionaries. Sadat resolved personally to set up an organisation of likeminded officers. As it happened, the two young officers who were to emerge as the most important members of the nucleus of revolutionaries were both marked out by their peculiar social habits: Sadat, who forsook social life to spend his leisure reading; and Nasser, whose solitary preferences distinguished him from his colleagues. But the establishment of an organisation calls for a certain amount of gregariousness, and Sadat identified his future comrades by engaging fellow officers in conversation and steering the topic round to the question of the power of the British military mission and the shame of Egyptian officers in having to acquiesce in the foreigners' demands. In 1938 Sadat and Zakariya Muhiaddin got their first posting together: to Manqabad in Upper Egypt. Their paths would converge later. Muhiaddin was to lead the drive for liberalisation from within 'Arab Socialist' Egypt. His friendship was crucial to Sadat when, on Nasser's death, they both felt excluded from the inner circles of power. In helping him seize Nasser's mantle, he may have eased Sadat towards the liberal, 'western' path pursued thereafter. In the early days, when Sadat and Muhiaddin were working together, a group of their friends began to acquire an informal structure, meeting for discussions in

Sadat's room in the remote garrison. In 1939, when Sadat was in the Signals Corps at Maada and greatly extending his contacts, the group constituted itself as a secret revolutionary society, the kernel — though not yet under the name — of the Free Officers' Organisation [Sadat, 1957, 13-14]. The society was built up rapidly, urgently, in the expectation that war would create a sudden opportunity to expel the British.

Sadat prized his own claim to priority over Nasser as founder of the Free Officers. While Nasser lived and controlled the output of historical myth in Egypt, Sadat went along with the official line and exalted his leader as *fons et origo* of the movement. He needed Nasser, for whom he anyway felt a genuinely awestruck admiration. Later, Nasser's death unmuzzled him and Sadat asserted his claim. The question is perhaps rather barren of interest except to those personally involved. Both men made essential contributions to the creation of the movement, which emerged as a process, not in a single act of foundation. Sadat's was the initial impulse, which Nasser crystallised and controlled in its crucial phase.

At that time and indeed up to — and even beyond — the revolution, the inchoate Free Officers had no real common ideology. Rather, they shared a passion to expel the British and make Egypt a strong and proud nation again. They were not yet even hostile to the monarchy. In Sadat's recollections of these early years, *Revolt on the Nile,* published in 1957, no animosity is evinced towards the monarchy as such; rather, Sadat sees Farouk as 'synonymous with patriotic idea' until he began to degenerate under the influence of the British coup of 1942. But in retrospect, Sadat identified half a dozen principles which were at the core of the Free Officers' hopes for Egypt: the elimination of imperialism and its supporters; the extirpation of feudalism and the liberation of the government from control by capitalists; the establishment of social justice; the raising of a strong national army and the creation of sound democratic life. They were dedicated, as he explained at the time to Hassan Banna of the Muslim Brotherhood, to overthrowing the existing British hegemony without adopting any specific vision of the precise political structure of the future [Sadat, 1957, 44].

The outbreak of the Second World War raised the prospect of ridding Egypt of the British. The proto-Free Officers were one of many loosely knit nationalist and revolutionary groups working towards the same end, with a more or less common figurehead and focus of loyalty in General Aziz al-Masry, the Egyptian army Chief of Staff who had first met Sadat and his friends at Manqabad during a tour of inspection before he was removed from active service in August 1940. Masry was unquestionably a brilliant officer, loyal to Egypt and not readily given to plotting against the government. But the Egyptian leadership in the war years — first under Ali Mahir's unrepresentative cabinet of King's Friends, then under a Wafdist régime that had 'sold out' to the British — failed to give an adequate lead to national feeling. Patriotic individuals were left to fend for themselves. Masry resolved to collaborate with the Axis powers for two reasons: first, for the sake of the principal objective, the expulsion of the British, and secondly, to prevent an Axis invasion of Egypt in the event of a British collapse, such as appeared imminent until 1943.

In deciding to help him, Sadat's mood was in keeping with that of the people who cried, 'Long live Rommel!' on the streets of Cairo. The king himself, who hated the British hegemony, and the very ministers who had been placed and maintained in power by force of British arms shared similar sentiments; late in 1942, even prime minister Nahas was trying to establish clandestine communications with Rommel. The trial of Masry and other officers in 1941 for attempting to reach the Axis lines was thus replete with irony and farce. Sadat had been privy to the abortive plot; he continued to help Masry maintain German contacts; but for much of 1941 and 1942 he and the members of his group were thrown back on their own devices to take action with Rommel. The Axis offensive of May 1942, which brought the Afrika Corps to the very threshold of Egypt, made the task urgent, if an invasion were to be averted, and the young officers took the first step in which they envisaged themselves as playing a quasi-governmental role by attempting to negotiate with Rommel — albeit unsuccessfully — on the part of the Egyptian people.

In October of that year Sadat's involvement with German agents embroiled him in the indiscretions which brought him to prison. Again, the drama was mixed with farce. By Sadat's account the Germans, Hans or 'Hussein' Eppler, or Abler, and an agent known to Sadat only as 'Sandy', lacked both dedication and competence. Their conception of their duty was contemptible. They seemed concerned only to spin out their assignment in inactivity, save among the brothels and bars. Like all bad workmen, they blamed their tools, alleging deficiencies in their transmitting equipment, which it would have been childishly simple to remedy. Their way of life was disgusting, for a moral as well as a professional point of view, and the obligation to work with them must have been distasteful to Sadat even in those young days before the full rigour of sententiousness infused his character. As it happened, restoring their ability to transmit was the only operation he had an opportunity to carry out with them. Their conspicuous self-indulgence betrayed them, in the person of a garrulous whore whom they had the bad taste to patronise. Their resistance to interrogation proved as fragile as to other forms of temptation. Sadat was arrested and sent to gaol in October 1942.

The episode of the two Germans nicely illustrates two features of all Sadat's dealing with the security authorities: his ingenuity under interrogation and the impression made on him by British respect for the rule of law. He broke down the testimony of Eppler and all the charges against himself and his fellow Free Officer, Hassan Izzat, before the Examining Council that preceded a trial. When the authorities tricked his father into trying to induce him to confess, he spotted the ruse. His close relationship of mutual confidence with his father enabled him to smooth over the episode. His quick eye for an interrogator's ploy, the perfection with which he concocted a story and the resolution with which he stuck to it probably saved his life on this occasion, though it could not save him from detention under wartime emergency regulations. He had already shown similar aptitude at the time of Masry's trial, when he extricated himself from danger by admitting all the verifiable facts but contriving to suggest explanations that were at once plausible and innocent. Later, when he was arrested again after the assassination of Amin Osman, he would once more put the same gifts to good use.

It may seem curious that Sadat, whose reputation for probity in politics is unequalled, should have been such a machiavel in custody. During the Amin Osman case, he falsely accused his interrogators of torturing him in order to assist his defence, even impugning warders of the Aliens' Gaol with whom he had become friendly during his previous incarceration. He mercilessly broke down fellow conspirators who had made confessions by deftly exploiting emotions during interrogation sessions. He almost perfected an art of counter-interrogation. It was an impressively proficient display of coolness under duress which only a man of tremendous character resources could have sustained. It was also cold-blooded and calculating. It showed how Sadat had the mental resourcefulness to step outside his own character when necessity demanded or danger threatened, to fight the world with worldly weapons. But he never felt that it compromised his integrity. Partly, he seems to have believed that the cause in which he was fighting sanctified falsehood; partly, that while Egypt was still in effect a British dependency, there was no validity in the judicial process and therefore every reason to undermine it.

In addition to his work with Masry and with German agents in the early war years, Sadat had actually formed an abortive insurrection plan to coincide with the Egyptian army's withdrawal from coastal and border installations in 1941. But it came to nothing. For the rest he was occupied with responsibilities as liaison between the protean Free Officers and the Muslim Brotherhood. His contact in that organisation was its founder, Hassan Al-Banna himself, the Supreme Guide whose command over the brethren was absolute. As a result of their meetings, Sadat became convinced that Islam could be mobilised as a revolutionary force, but not under the aegis of the dangerous and dictatorial shaikh. He was fully engaged in resisting Al-Banna's rather contrived charisma and the entanglements of the tentacular *Ikhwan*, which aspired to control all revolutionary groups. As he informed Masry, ''I told Sheikh Al-Banna from the start that we work for Egypt, not for any party or bloc.'' [Sadat, 1978, 26].

In fact, in these years, Sadat's circle of friends were gradually moving towards the establishment of a formal, independent organisation of their own, with a network spread throughout the armed forces and, indeed, throughout the nation. In 1942, the secret organisation formed in 1939 was reorganised into sections within the army, the sections dispersed around the various units and garrisons. When Sadat was arrested, the work proceeded, first under Abdul Munaim Abdul-Rauf, with Nasser emerging by 1943 as the leader and co-ordinator in Sadat's absence. The central core of friends from Manqabad still seem to have exerted a predominant influence and it was they who raised a subsistence of £10 per month for Sadat's wife and children while he was in gaol. A further reorganisation took place in 1944 or early 1945 into a military group headed by Nasser and a popular group, placed on his emergence from prison under Sadat's command, though its existence was shadowy as yet [Sadat, 1957, 13-14, 56; 1978, 57].

There is a kind of tragic irony in the fact that Sadat was so closely identified at the start of his revolutionary career with the very brand of Muslim fanaticism that would later decree his own death. It is ironic, too, that the very organisation with which he worked, the Muslim Brotherhood, should have spawned the fundamentalist factions to which his own assassins later belonged. And it is ironic, finally, that he should have been a practitioner and — as we shall see — an apologist of the same methods of political assassination as would later prove his own undoing. Like his improbable friend, Menachem Begin of Israel, he was a terrorist converted by success to statesmanship. It seems unlikely that the mean vision of his murderers will ever effect a similar transformation in them.

But, for the present, prison was the only setting available for his talents: first, the Aliens' Gaol, then a gilded cage in the Maqusah Palace near Al-Minya, which had been converted to a detention centre; then, from November 1943, Zaytun in Cairo. By the time he reached this last location, he was restless and uncontainable. He embarked on a campaign of insubordination and mutiny, before resorting, with Hassan Izzat and a few other friends, to escape, not in the first instance with the object of regaining liberty but simply as a gesture of defiance and a protest against the conduct of the life of the prison by its authorities. While the other escapers made good their flight, he and Muhsin Fadil made their point by returning to Zaytun, after pausing ostentatiously at the Abdin Palace to sign the Royal Ceremonies Book, and causing enough embarrassment and shock to bring about a shake-up in the prison service.

By October 1944, with the war in Egypt over and the end of the general war in sight, Sadat's exasperation with prison reached breaking-point. A hunger strike saw him transferred to military hospital, whence escape, with Hassan Izzat's help, was easy. On the run for more than a year, Sadat was dedicated to survival, without leisure to spare for revolutionary work. Changing identities and adopting a beard as a disguise, he worked as a lorry driver, a navvy, and a transport contractor to earn enough to live on.

Sadat's fugitive days ended with the war. The abrogation of martial law meant that he was free to emerge from hiding. He exploited his liberty to get on with the task of building a popular organisation to complement the proto-Free Officers and to plot the elimination of the pro-British collaborators, Saadists and Wafdists alike, who still controlled the state. This was an aim shared by nationalists in parliament and across the nation; Sadat was only one of a host of individuals, his friends only one among many organisations, all devoted to seeking the same ends, some by constitutional, some by revolutionary means. For instance, the hated Wafdist premier, Mustapha al-Nahas, who had made nonsense of Wafdist tradition by seizing and clinging to power solely by virtue of British connivance, had been constitutionally unseated in October 1944. His successor, the Saadist Ahmad Mahir, was assassinated by an Ikhwan fanatic at the inauguration of a long campaign of terrorism by the Brethren, in February 1945. There were demonstrations and general strikes involving hundreds of thousands of Egyptians in the first three months of 1946. It was against this background that the next decisive event of Sadat's career, the assassination of Amin Osman, took place.

The execution was preceded in December 1945 by an unsuccessful attempt by Sadat and the same team on the life of Mustapha Nahas, with Sadat training the assassins in the use of hand grenades. It was thought at the time to be the work of the Ikhwan: Sadat has since revealed the small, *ad hoc* nature of the group that coalesced to perform the deed [Sadat, 1978, 58]. Most of them had strong brotherhood connections: their escapades can only be understood in the context of the widespread violence the Brethren promoted at that time. The Ikhwan had an adoptive attitude towards Sadat and paid maintenance to his family as well — it is to be presumed — as his lawyers' fees when he was arrested for his part in the plot. Of Nahas's tergiversation and general qualifications for assassination enough has been said (above p. 17). Amin Osman's misfortune was genuinely to love a race most of his countrymen had reason to detest. His anglophilia was of the intensity and malignity of a disease. The war had dispelled the admiration for England of most Egyptian intellectuals: British strength had been exposed as a myth, British liberalism as a sham. Men like Taha Husayn and Muhammad Husain Haykal responded positively to these lessons of the war: not so, however, Osman, who had no wish even to alleviate the degree of Egyptian dependence on Britain. He was tainted with the opprobrium of the Wafd's conversion in 1942 from a nationalist to a pro-British line, for he had acted as liaison between Nahas and the British ambassador. Now, an unrepentant anglophile, he was Minister of Finance.

Sadat's part in his assassination in January 1946 was instrumental, but its exact nature is not yet known. Assassination was a course he generally opposed: later he was to restrain Nasser from launching the Free Officers' revolutionary campaign with a series of homicides [Sadat, 1978, 102]; it was a weapon of the Ikhwan, of which he wanted no part; it was unsoldierly. After the event, Sadat was acquitted of complicity, despite the British authorities' private certainty of his guilt; and later, in 1957, he referred to the proof of his innocence of the charge [Sadat, 1957, 74]. But he was always popularly regarded as responsible and in his recent reminiscences he made it clear that the popular opinion is correct.

It seems curious that Sadat's pride should have grown over the years in what was arguably a discreditable episode. Association with a terrorist past might have seemed more appropriate for the soldier-revolutionary of 1957, when he published *Revolt on the Nile,* than for the statesman and peacemaker of 1978. Yet Sadat concealed the truth of his murderous past at the earlier date, and confessed it at the later. More surprisingly still, he used the occasion of his memoirs to vindicate the practice of political assassination in a revolutionary cause, at a time when he knew himself to be the target of revolutionary assassins. The only convincing explanation of this apparent paradox is that in 1978 the president was making a genuine confession, in an almost religious sense. An undiscriminating passion for truth compelled him to put the record right, even in the case of an episode which had neither merit nor advantage — only danger and obloquy — for him. A truth as terrible as that of complicity in the Osman assassination had to await propitious circumstances, but at last there came a moment when he could no longer withhold it.

He was in gaol on remand until July 1948, and so missed the start of the Palestinian War. His civilian wing of the officers' movement had fallen inoperative. He spent the next eighteen months adrift — the first few weeks recovering from prison life in a crumbling Hilwan *pension,* from which Hassan Izzat rescued him. Finding commercial life, trading with the Saudis via Suez, not to his taste, he got a journalistic job on *Al-Hilal* before returning to business, working once again with his friend, Hassan Izzat, on water supply contracts. Though he liked the journalism and found he had a talent for it, he yearned to rejoin the army, especially as he resented having missed the fighting against Israel in the first Arab-Israeli war of 1948. Business, moreover, revolted him. He hated the quibbles over profit-sharing with his partner and the thought of spending his whole life in such an arid occupation appalled him.

The only positive step forward of this period of his life was meeting and marrying his second wife, Jihan. She was Hassan Izzat's cousin and Sadat met her through his partner. His first marriage had been dissolved, after his second imprisonment, on his initiative because, in a sense, he had outgrown it. He still felt he belonged to his village past; he had no wish to reject his peasant background. But the spiritual awakening he underwent in prison so extended the limits of his life that the narrow and conventional framework of his marriage could no longer contain them. His first wife was unable to understand his way of life, discuss with him the principles that guided it, or share in the dangers and adventures in which it consisted. He had choked back as disloyal and disgusting an earlier fancy for an educated wife [Sadat, 1978, 74], but in prison he came to the conviction that it was unrealistic to face the future in unchanged domestic circumstances.

It had not been a romantic match and certainly not an intellectual one, but a routine village marriage between distant cousins, contracted and arranged by mutual custom when the spouses were mere children. In the vocation of war and revolution he had chosen, Sadat needed a more dynamic helpmate. In exercising the intellectual powers he had discovered in himself he needed a more brilliant wife. He was fortunate to find in Jihan a woman who combined intellectual distinction, social and political commitment, a dynamic talent, and a modesty and morality that enabled her to exercise all her gifts within the traditional Islamic prescription of a wife's role. They married for love. But each found in the other an ideal partner for life. For both of them the marriage was an astonishing act of faith, a spectacular assertion of courage in adversity. Anwar somehow perceived the qualities that were still maturing in the young woman. Jihan somehow appreciated the steadfastness and sense of purpose that had been temporarily frustrated in the man.

Within eight months of his marriage to Jihan, Sadat was back in the army, arguing plausibly that since he had been found not guilty in the Osman affair there was no call to exclude him from his commission. But he had lost pay and promotion and, more important, he had missed significant developments in the officers' movement amid the general intensification of revolutionary activity in these years. Immediately on his reinstatement Sadat received a telephone call from Nasser, who brought him up to date on the spread of the movement in the army and air force. He felt he could so easily have been excluded from the leadership — he was the only one of the central core of friends not to have served in the Palestinian war, his periods of incarceration had handicapped his work for the movement; he had been out of the army at a crucial time. He was therefore touched by Nasser's loyalty in including him at the meeting of the nine members who formed the constitutent council of the movement and took the name of Free Officers, later that month. But it was not mere friendship that actuated Nasser: he was also aware of the usefulness, indeed the necessity, of Sadat's inclusion, as a revolutionary of unexcelled ability and sincerity, who knew all the leading Free Officers well, had brought many of them together in the first instance, and had, in fact, been the *primum mobile* of the movement and an essential part of it since its inception. Moreover, Sadat's rumoured role in the Amin Osman affair made him popularly celebrated.

Nasser was enigmatic in his friendships: one has only to think of his tempestuous relationship with Abdul Hakim Amer, whose every indiscretion and excess he condoned until this 'friend' turned to open enmity, to appreciate that. With Sadat, Nasser's relationship was unquestionably one of the deepest friendship, formed with a bond which both men felt to be unbreakable. But it had a similarly inscrutable element. In the approximately eighteen months of active preparation that preceded the Free Officers' seizure of power, the two were boon companions, spending five days out of seven together. And Nasser was not ungenerous in acknowledging Sadat's contribution to the revolution when at last it came. In 1957 he was to write in his foreword to Sadat's *Revolt on the Nile*,

> [Sadat's] military virtues, courage and coolness, loyalty and
> devotion, force of character and disinterestedness and finally

his love of justice, destined him to play a leading role in the Egyptian revolution of July 23rd, 1952 [Sadat, 1957, viii].

But the period of preparation in '50-52 was arguably the closest phase of the two leaders' association. They planned the revolution together, but Nasser no longer demanded the same quality of companionship from his friend once it was under way. For instance, Sadat was surprised to find himself attacked by Nasser and Salah Salim in the Revolutionary Command Council, learning only later that this was because of his popularity as the hero of the Osman affair. Whereas his advice had generally been heeded in the pre-July period, when he suggested in 1953 that conflicts in the council might be resolved by demanding the resignation of dissident members, he found Nasser 'strangely bitter' and 'vituperative' [Sadat, 1978, 102]. When Nasser took the helm of the nation, he behaved as if he felt threatened by Sadat, whose willingness to serve in subordinate or nominal positions gratified him. The important missions he confided to Sadat were those of conciliation and pacification, smoothing over personal animosities within the ranks of the council, patching up understandings with America or Iran whenever a characteristically hot-headed speech had disturbed relations.

In addition to his frequent planning sessions with Nasser, Sadat was active in the field in the pre-revolutionary period, training and supplying *fedayeen*. A revolutionary situation was taking shape. Government reforms since the war — progressive taxation, re-codification of the law, legislation in favour of trades unions, sickness compensation, distribution of land to peasants — had been such as to titillate but not satisfy the popular appetite. The army was rife with disillusionment after its failures in Palestine for which, with some justice, the corruption and incompetence of the administration was blamed; it was this mood that fuelled the rapid progress of the Free Officers. The fall in *per capita* income mobilised the classes on whom the burden fell, as strikes and demonstrations continued. Above all, anti-British feeling seemed to be fired rather than assuaged by the partial withdrawal of troops to the Canal Zone. This whetted Egyptian demands for the total ejection of the imperialists. At the same time, British delays and denials over the Egyptian government's proposal to re-negotiate the pre-war friendship treaty between the two governments further inflamed opinion and led to the unilateral abrogation of the treaty in May 1950.

Sadat had expected and planned for a revolution in perhaps about five years' time, but in the deteriorating situation of 1950-51 he and Nasser kept their plans flexible. The details of the timing are uncertain. Sadat's recollection in 1957, in *Revolt on the Nile,* had changed twenty years later when he wrote *In Search of Identity* [Sadat, 1957, 107]. In the event it was the government's inability to manage relations with Britain that precipitated the insurrection in 1952. For some time, fedayeen of the sort Sadat had helped to train had been operating against British bases, officially uncountenanced but effectively unimpeded by the ministers of the Egyptian crown. As guerrilla operations intensified, so did British counter-measures, and so did national feeling and popular outrage at governmental impotence increase. The government could neither control the guerrillas themselves — they lacked the will — nor prevent or even oppose British retaliation — they lacked the force. They remained spectators of an even bloodier and more chaotic battle, in the course of which British incursions bit ever deeper into Egyptian territory as the guerrillas were harried and pursued to their bases. The fighting culminated in the Ismailiyya incident of January 25th, 1952, when, on government orders, Egyptian soldiers and police resisted a British advance and sustained over fifty fatal casualties. The result was a sudden outburst of long pent-up public disorder — violence, arson and mob rule. Six months of anarchical ministerial instability ensued.

Meanwhile the Free Officers had established a hold on the loyalties of the armed forces. In December 1951 the candidates they sponsored were elected to the Presidency and Board of Directors of the Officers' Club, with General Muhammad Naguib, the senior army man to sympathise with the revolutionaries, at their head. Thus success, achieved despite the declared hostility of the king, convinced King Farouk that the army was potentially seditious and had to be controlled directly by the crown. He therefore kept independent ministries in power, neglecting the vital need for a basis of support among the parliamentary parties, merely in order to keep the defence ministry in the hands of a creature. This situation, intolerable to the armed forces, unacceptable to the politicians and irrelevant to the needs of the people, decided the Free Officers in favour of an early date for the uprising. Sadat already knew from his friend Yusuf Rashad, who had the king's ear, that Farouk was intimidated and demoralised; there was no likelihood of opposition from any other source within the country. The British, who had foiled the army's last attempt to spearhead a popular revolution in 1882, were now relatively powerless and had no vital interest in the composition of Egypt's government. There was thus no real obstacle to the fulfilment of his plans.

The occasion came so suddenly that even Sadat was taken by surprise. A posthumously published article of Sadat's has added considerably to what was known of the immediate circumstances of the revolution from his early writings (which were often obscure and mutually contradictory) and from the accounts of other participants. The conspirators expected, at the beginning of 1952, to launch their attempt the following November: in the summer, when the seat of government was in Alexandria, while the permanent institutions of the state remained in Cairo, a revolt would be doubly hazardous. The 'Cairo fire' of January, the increasing level of popular anxiety and, finally, the decisive events of July first advanced and then precipitated the revolutionaries' plans. On 22nd July, following the fall of the fifth government since the Ismailiyya incident, Naguib Hilali was re-appointed to the premiership. The Free Officers thought that Hussain Sirry — a 'tough' candidate pledged to extirpate dissent, would get the war ministry. 'We feared that he would round us up and abort our revolution.' Thus with the first rumours of the possible composition of the new government, Nasser decided to act pre-emptively: 'If we wait, Hussain Sirry will destroy us. We have to eat him before he eats us.' In fact, the king imposed the choice of Ismail Sharin as war minister, but the orders for an insurrection had already gone out. (In any case, Ismail Sharin was hardly a popular choice, nor was the army generally pleased with royal interference.)

Sadat hurried to Cairo for the seizure of power with which the Free Officers were resolved to respond to the latest ministerial changes. Unable to find Nasser, as previously arranged, at the railway station on his arrival, he went to the cinema. This might have been an elusive measure; it might have been simple funk. In fact, Sadat's posthumous article makes it apparent that it was merely a mistake. Having missed his fellow revolutionaries, and detecting no sign of impending rebellion, he assumed that the insurrection had been postponed once again. Emerging from the cinema after sitting through three consecutive films and a forty-five minute electrical breakdown, Sadat found a series of messages from Nasser. Following these up, he eventually encountered Amer, who was able to brief him on how events were unfolding. By this time, the revolutionaries were already celebrating their success. A series of comic accidents, culminating in Sadat's inability to get past the Free Officers' own pickets, had prevented him from witnessing the most dramatic moments of the coup he had worked for and planned for so long. The army headquarters were occupied late on the night of the 22nd and senior officers of doubtful loyalties arrested by the insurrectionists. Sadat was put in charge of the revolutionary troops manning army headquarters while other units loyal to the Free Officers took over the H.Q. of the frontier force and all major centres of communications. At seven o'clock the next morning, it was Sadat's voice that announced the events of the night to the people. Not for the last time, the sound of his voice over the air was an occasion of popular rejoicing [Mayo, 17th August, 1982].

From Sadat's point of view, the story of the revolution up to the time of his presidency was a tale of endeavour and disillusionment. Almost at once, his hopes and expectations began to crumble. He had wanted 'a healthy political life' for the country, without the king, without the British, without the political factions, but with continuous civilian government. By August 1952, however, worsening civil unrest — much of it whipped up by the Ikhwan, resentful of the Free Officers' resistance to theocratic tutelage, had brought about violent strikes which had to be repressed; in September the civilian government refused to implement the agrarian reforms demanded by the revolutionaries with wholesale redistribution of land to the peasants. On September 7th the officers therefore reluctantly took on the government's role themselves.

Muhammad Naguib headed what was still a civilian cabinet, but from this moment the officers were effectively and increasingly the real government of the country [Sadat, 1978, 123]. Even more distressing to Sadat were the dissensions that broke out in the ranks of the Revolutionary Command Council. These were in a sense to be expected, since the council included men as far to the left as Khalid Muhiaddin, constitutionalists like Naguib, and officers who sympathised or had sympathised with the Ikhwan and even Young

Egypt. But to Sadat, the power struggles and continual reshuffling of the council's personnel appeared as signs of the corrupting effects of power, rather than clashes of principle [Sadat, 1978, 126]. He was in no position to exercise personal influence. He was dependent on Nasser, who was happy to keep him subservient, on the sidelines, well away from any post in which he could rebuild the authority he possessed in the early days of the Free Officers.

Sadat stood apart from the struggles. His personal role in 1953 was a judicial one as a member of the tribunal established to try members of the old régime accused of corruption. After the worst period of factional squabbles within the council in 1954, he became a member of the People's Court, set up to try treasonable elements, mostly from within the Ikhwan, who had attempted to assassinate Nasser and had contrived an extensive plot against the revolution. But throughout this period he was trying to withdraw from the centre of the stage. He actually attempted resignation in 1953 and again in 1955 in protest at the conflicts among his colleagues; he was out of patience with the way Naguib insisted on treating him as a rival. He thought of emigrating to Lebanon, to escape into a world of natural beauty.

From December 1953 Sadat was at work on the establishment of his revolutionary newspaper, *Al-Gumhuriya,* which he was to serve in person as editor-in-chief, while accepting concurrently a junior government post as a minister of state. He continued to make policy contributions — arguing strongly, for instance, in favour of the Evacuation Agreement with Britain of 1954, which at last rid Egyptian soil of British troops after three-quarters of a century of occupation, and using his post as Secretary of the Islamic Congress to help frustrate the Baghdad Pact in January 1955. But his heart was no longer in the business of government. Politicking repelled him almost as much as commerce had done. When Nasser was elected president in the plebiscite of June, 1956, and a period of stability for the Free Officer régime at last seemed at hand, Sadat asked not to be included in the new ministry.

He played no direct part in the Suez crisis in 1956. He was a passive participant in the national exultation Egyptians felt on hearing their leader tell the western powers to 'choke on their rage' and 'drink the Mediterranean': it was a moment of great pride. As editor of *Al-Gumhuriya,* Sadat helped government policy along with a series of attacks on the American Secretary of State, John Foster Dulles; for it must be remembered that the real *casus belli* of the Suez crisis was American refusal to help Egypt with the Aswan Dam project. The Suez Canal Company and the British and French governments simply suffered the backlash of general Egyptian disenchantment with the west.

Sadat was unwavering in his public support for every Egyptian action in the Suez affair but was candid about the fact that he had private reservations. He admitted that, had he been in a position to influence events, he would have advised against the gamble of nationalising the canal company, on the grounds that Egypt was not ready for war. Of course he was delighted, as all Egypt was, that despite his misgivings the gamble paid off. But the imprudence of it perturbed him [Sadat, 1978, 143]. In the years after 1956, in Egypt, the real perils of the Suez adventure were forgotten in the euphoria; the myth spread that Egypt's victory had been a military one, whereas it was in fact only American diplomatic intervention that saved Egypt from a devastating defeat. The unpreparedness of the armed forces was borne out by Israeli battlefield successes in Sinai and Egyptian impotence to stop the Anglo-French occupation of the canal zone.

Suez was a culmination. There followed a period in the history of the revolution which Sadat has called 'ten years of sleep' [Israeli, 87]. He devoted himself to his writing and, as Deputy Speaker and Speaker of the National Assembly, to parliamentary affairs. Until about 1961, this was a time of domestic contentment for Sadat and hope for the nation. Suez euphoria was still in the air. Federation with Syria in 1958 brought new prospects as well as new problems. Sadat was able to get on with the journalism he loved and had time for more substantial writing as well as for broadcasts in which he extolled traditional values.

Sadat published *Revolt on the Nile* in 1957, in which he threaded historical narrative with personal reminiscence: the result was an original piece of literature, richly evocative, fast-moving and vivid. Then followed his pen portrait of Nasser, *My Son, This is your Uncle Gamal,* in which he explored the fraternal love he felt for Nasser, despite their political differences. It was apparent that he valued love and all personal feelings above political opinions. The undogmatic humanity for which he was renowned — and perhaps unique — in world politics was already a fully formed part of his character by the time he wrote this book.

The adulatory tone of *My Son, This is your Uncle Gamal* is embarrassing to western readers. It is a hagiography in the oriental tradition. Its author's critical faculties are suspended. The twists and sharp angles in the subject's character, refracted through the lens of pious admiration, appear smooth and straight. It is not surprising that Sadat wrote about his boss in a fawning, almost cringing manner. He had no choice, nor, at the time, had he any other desire. Sadat was never hesitant in hero-worship or temperate in enthusiasm. Everything he espoused was embraced without restraint. While Nasser lived, he was enthralled by him and responded wholeheartedly to the leader's allure. Only later could Sadat reconsider the relationship in something like detachment.

At the beginning of the 'sixties a change overcame Egypt and Sadat's mood and even his health changed with it. All the changes were for the worse. His health suffered a blow when, after chairing the Afro-Asian Solidarity Conference in Conakry in May 1960, he was struck by a heart attack. He passed it off as caused by overwork and the uncongenial Guinean climate; but it was the strain of enduring the atmosphere of intrigue and suspicion in Cairo, rather than the honest toridity of Conakry, that afflicted him. He had already resigned the chairmanship of Egypt's quasi-party organisation, the National Union. The feeling that the revolution was turning sour was confirmed as the year drew on, while, as the newly elected Speaker of the National Assembly of the United Arab Republic, Sadat saw Syrian-Egyptian unity founder on Syrian resentment.

The break-up of the union did not surprise Sadat: he had been convinced by King Faisal's private prophecy of just such an outcome. But it was still a source of disappointment. Worse yet was the degeneracy of government within Egypt, as Amer and other wielders of personal power challenged one another, and even Nasser himself. There is no need to recount these extinct monsters' struggles here: Sadat, to his credit, took no part in them. Nasser summarised them adequately to Sadat when he said that the country was being run 'by a gang of thieves' [Sadat, 1978, 168]. This was the decade of the vicious corruption of Amer's Committee for the Liquidation of Feudalism, the worst deprivations of elementary liberty by Salah Nasr's secret police, and the bloody imbecilities of the Yemeni war, which Sadat later deplored but for which he was justly obliged to bear political responsibility.

This piece of knight-errantry appealed to his romanticism and idealism; he urged intervention on Nasser and it may well be that but for the intensity of his pleading the fateful decision to embroil Egypt in the Yemen adventure would never have been taken. Curiously, the failure in the Yemen cemented the relationship of Nasser and Sadat. Their mutual affection was renewed; they emerged from the imbroglio, allies and friends, without yielding to the temptation to indulge in recriminations. The episode probably helped Nasser to see Sadat as an acceptable heir. Though Sadat subsequently felt ashamed of the Yemeni aberration and tried to obscure his part in it, it was in fact for him a fruitful failure, which eased his path to the presidency.

The end product of the ten years' sleep was the June War of 1967. This is not the place to retrace the events surrounding that traumatic episode. But its effects on Sadat and the lessons he drew from it are vital to an understanding of his statecraft. Egypt's part in precipitating the war was, as Sadat came to realise, the result of an irrational collective impulse. Abdel Hakim Amer misled other decision-makers about the level of readiness of the armed forces but, even so, it was apparent to any objective scrutineer that war would be a risky business. Yet Egyptians rushed to the front like lemmings, some plunging, some merely foundering, fixed in the delusion that a once-for-all trial with Israel was at hand.

This experience was not wasted on Sadat. He realised, after the war was lost, that the next round of fighting would have to be carefully prepared over a long time and that the political leadership would have to take an active interest in the planning. When he led Egypt to war in 1973, none of the old mistakes was repeated. Battle was joined calculatingly, not merely impetuously; Sadat himself had looked into the state of the armed forces and had watched over and contributed to the elaboration of strategy.

There were other, equally important lessons to be gained from 1967. Sadat felt strongly that Nasser should have taken personal command, not only because he was convinced of the incompetence and unreliability of Amer, but also because he thought the broader national interest demanded it. When he became president himself, he never shirked responsibility for any major area of national endeavour. And he noticed one source of comfort to be salvaged from the '67 débâcle: the circumstances of war had a beneficial effect on national morale: here was another lesson to be stored for the future.

Sadat's own response to the disasters of that June was deeply — even uncharacteristically — emotional. Normally possessed of great self-control, given to ratiocination, adept at pragmatism, Sadat was a man whose emotions were rarely engaged, but when they were, they were wholeheartedly. The emotional climax came with the news that the Israelis had conquered Sinai and were poised on the canal's bank. He assumed that they would cross to Egypt's heartland: this itself shows how he had cast political sophistication aside in his grief and wrath, since broad considerations of international politics were virtually certain to detain the Israelis in Sinai. He took his rifle and 'drove away to fight my own battle'. As Speaker of the National Assembly, he called for the activation of plans for local small-war resistance to the enemy. He telephoned Nasser to advise him to withdraw to Upper Egypt and be a focus for national resistance there, like Gambetta hot-air ballooning to the Loire during France's national trauma a hundred years before.

Yet despite all this, Sadat was one of the few Egyptians whose personal morale seemed to survive the 1967 catastrophe. He drew encouragement from the gradual recovery of the Egyptian armed forces and the boost to morale derived from the start of the War of Attrition in September 1968. Nasser, meanwhile, was a broken man, his health and spirit wrecked: the last three years of his life were wretched, the early end foreseeable to those who knew him well. Amer, who bore so much personal responsibility for the defeat, was, if anything, even more seriously affected. The precarious balance of his always febrile brain had been menaced by disaster. His plots against Nasser were born of despair, not hope. Sadat tried to befriend him, not because he approved — far from it — of anything Amer had done in recent years, but because he hoped to dissuade the adventurer from any rash escapade and get him to try to rebuild a useful life. But Amer's response to friendly overtures was paranoid; his plotting intensified. When arrest provoked him into suicide, Nasser was sincerely grief-stricken, but Sadat said openly that it was for the best [Sadat, 1978, 193]. Amer had belonged to a phase of the history of the revolution Sadat believed and hoped was ending.

On December 28th, 1970, Sadat told the *New York Times* that he had been appointed to the vice-presidency because Nasser had a presentiment of death. Certainly, Nasser's decline after the defeat of 1967 was perceptible to Sadat as it was to many observers. He was so physically enfeebled, so morally debilitated, that he was incapable of resisting death. And it is possible that he turned to his long-time friend as the only potential successor who would not alienate any major faction or be unacceptable to any part of the population. But there were few who believed that Sadat could be more than a temporary, stop-gap, compromise-candidate president.

He had always deliberately sought the background; that was in part why he was so widely acceptable; he had never pursued power or evinced ambition: that gave him ironic credibility in his rivals' eyes. He had never dabbled in the extra-constitutional power-bloc-building common in Nasser's entourage and so possessed no network of patronage, no gaggle of clients, no squad of bully-boys to help keep him in office. He could expect little co-operation from Egypt's sullen, flatulent bureaucracy. He could count on the covetousness of many colleagues: Ali Sabry, who wanted to wrench state policy back to a pro-Soviet line; Mahmud Fawzi, whose overweening ambition would shortly be revealed; Zakaria Muhiaddin, who was widely regarded as Nasser's adopted heir; Sharawi Gomaa, who believed he could control Sadat and was enraged to find the president had a will of his own.

These men were widely famed or notorious, favoured and feared. Sadat, not intent on power for himself, had not courted fame; he was well known mainly among the intellectual élite who read his journalism or books or followed the work he had done on the parliamentary and international stages in recent years. Similarly, he had not tried ever to inspire fear: respect was the only kindred emotion he evoked. The story goes that his photograph was unrecognisable to inhabitants of Cairo at the time of Nasser's death. It was not realised that his obscurity derived not from a lack of ability but from strength of character. It was not appreciated that the most prominent reputations in Egypt after 1967 were also the most vulnerable, or that resolution and integrity would count for more in the next few years than claques of clients. In the things that mattered, Sadat had an advantage over his rivals.

If at the time of his assumption of the presidency his personal position was dismissed as precarious by the pundits, the situation — economic and political — of Egypt seemed even more doom-fraught. It was expected that the problems would defeat him, even if his enemies did not. A few years later, Sadat summed up the array of difficulties with which he was confronted:

"Nasser, my friend and brother, left an inheritance to me: our relations with the entire world...and with the Arab Nation were at their worst...He left me a military situation whereby Israel was positioned on the Canal Bank, and the Russians tormented him. It is true that he had no one but the Russians, after he had cut off his relations with the entire world...He also bequeathed to me a group of people, whose members scrambled for his succession. Economically, too, our situation had never been so bad...He also bequeathed to me the rancour that was widespread all over the country."
[Israeli, 1201-02]

In addition, the government's liquidity was laughable: Sadat feared that there would not be enough cash to pay state wages. And Egypt's agricultural exports were mortgaged for years ahead to Russia for arms. It was, Sadat said, an 'apparently insuperable' combination [Sadat, 1978, 103]. His problems were like a range of high mountains, of which the 1967 defeat formed the highest peak, while economic collapse and diplomatic isolation looked almost equally daunting. The bedrock was the legacy of misgovernment by some of Nasser's subordinates — some self-seeking, some corrupt, some merely sadistic: internal espionage had formed a 'mountain of hatred'; fear and mutual suspicion had devitalised the Egyptians [Sadat, 1978, 209]. The ordinary people felt excluded from decision-making that vitally affected them. Economic policies had contributed to national demoralisation; the government's borrowings from Marxism had not only led to economic disarray, they had also sapped enterprise and initiative and made people passive, even lackadaisical.

The Committee for the Liquidation of Feudalism sums up much that was worst about the 'sixties in Egypt. Its name was a Marxist euphemism concealing, Sadat had said, 'terror, repression and humiliation'; it was a means of power and corruption to Abdel Hakim Amer and his friends; the trials of some of them in 1968 drew attention to the prevalence of corrupt self-enrichment among men not far from the heart of the régime; it showed how narrow were the limits of liberty. Meanwhile, beneath the tension on the surface, inexorable population growth continued to inch Egyptians deeper into poverty.

But there were patches of hope in the bleak scene Sadat surveyed from the presidential residence at the end of this drastic decade. Nasser's last years had been marked, if by no discovery of solutions, at least by realisation of some of the problems. Sadat himself had identified many of the causes of Egypt's difficulties in the early 'fifties, when his dissatisfaction with the course of the revolution first began to make him restless. He had had plenty of time in which to contemplate and formulate some solutions of his own. And there were some developments which, rightly handled, could accrue to the country's advantage.

Nasser's death had united the nation in reverence of the memory of 'Abu Khalid' ('Father of Khalid', the name by which, by Arabic convention, Nasser was posthumously known). The extension of the cease-fire with Israel brought the first glimmer of a distant prospect of peace. Oil-production was increasing, as was that of rice. Finance was available for the Sumed pipeline. Among the Egyptian people, national sentiment was high. A mood of 'Egyptian first, Arab second' — which was well attuned to both the country's practical needs and the policies Sadat had in mind — was growing and deepening in intensity. The difficulties Sadat faced outweighed the opportunities. But at least the raw material was available on which his statecraft would work. He was like an architect obliged to build on a bomb-site, to reconstruct from ruins and rubble with only very limited access to new materials. It was against this background of problems that he entered on his years of achievement.

CHAPTER THREE

The Man Sadat

Faith

If we ask, 'What sort of man was Sadat?', we are really posing two questions: first, 'What was his perception of himself?', for Sadat was not a man to be influenced by other men's images; rather, the keynote of his career was loyalty to his own vision of himself, a refusal to be constrained by forces and agencies outside his control. Secondly, it is proper to ask how far an objective characterisation of him can be inferred from his writings and conduct; even a character as forceful as Sadat may not be able to project his own self-image onto the screen of events without distortion. We must allow for the possibility that our perception of the president may be different from his own.

In fact, if we compare these two perceptions — Sadat's self-image and the impression he made on observers — a discrepancy is immediately obvious. It is not a discrepancy of substance since, as we shall see, Sadat was remarkably (albeit not entirely) free of self-deception; he saw himself substantially as others see him. But it is a matter of priorities. In Sadat's own view he was first and foremost a peasant: this is the first fact about himself he revealed to readers of his reminiscenses; it is a theme to which he frequently returned in speeches; it was a role he performed sitting on the 'good earth' of his village, dispensing justice in a rustic *gallabiya.*

But it is not the element of his background which seems most essential, most fundamental to objective scrutiny. For a dispassionate onlooker, Sadat's basic ingredient — so to speak — was his faith. He was a peasant by origin, certainly, and to a great degree by preference; but his *nostalgie de la boue* is a reminder that the course of his life forced him in part away from his peasant origins. Like the limbs of a huge tree, his presidential responsibilities and preoccupations were joined to their roots — but only at a great distance. His peasant's nature always affected him, but it was not at the heart of his thoughts and actions, as his Islamic faith was. A content analysis of his speeches reveals that terms and images of religion contribute at least twice as much to his language as those of any other category. Without Islam, Sadat would be a dumb image, a fragment of clay which God had not yet inspired with the breath of speech.

In the context of the present essentially political study of Sadat, it is the political outflow of his faith that first draws attention. He defined politics as 'the art of building up a society wherein the will of God is enacted' [Sadat, 1978, 89]. It is a formula that takes westerners by surprise. They tend to regard it as archaic, 'medieval', because in the western tradition it has been assumed since the middle ages that politics and religion are distinct, without an overlap, that the spiritual and secular spheres constitute separate worlds. Such a dichotomy is meaningless in Islam, which is at once a system of beliefs, a way of life, and a body of precepts for the regulation and conduct of society. Thus Sadat's definition strikes a chord in the very heartstrings of Islam. But it left him, of course, with a problem of practical application.

As a political interpreter of his religion, Sadat distilled from this general conception of politics governed by faith a more precise social doctrine of human dignity and equality. For Islam is in many ways a more humanistic, more anthropocentric religion than Judaism or Christianity. Muslims believe strongly in the perfectibility of man, his special favour in the eyes of God; they view man's prospects of salvation without the jaundiced eye of the Jew or the hag-ridden conscience of the Christian; they are convinced of man's goodness, confident of his role. This makes them optimistic, on the whole, of man's chances of creating a just society and egalitarian in their social attitudes, as they contemplate the equality of all men before God.

Sadat's vision of a 'just society' for his region of the world was based on belief in the common humanity and equality of all men and the special mutual obligations of the co-religionists in Monotheism who live there. Nowhere in his works does this emerge more strongly than from his famous speech to the Israeli Knesset of November 1977: a third of this speech was devoted to what a western reader would identify as religious themes (though to Sadat, of course, they were inseparably religious and political all at once) and the divine nature of Sadat's conception of his peace mission shone through the exalted language [Salem-Babikian, 13, 18-21]. An Israeli deputy, watching the

Egyptian president almost aflame with intense spirituality, has remarked privately that it was like beholding a transfiguration.

Paradoxically, perhaps, while actively pursuing his vision and his mission, Sadat was influenced by a simpler political faith, too: the submissiveness which Islam demands to divine will, the resignation before fatalism which is characteristic of Islam. 'God created men to play the roles assigned to them', he says [Sadat, 1978, 76], and he was always scrutinising his own role in the light of prayer, Quranic study and meditation. No reader of his reminiscenses can fail to be struck by the strength and frequency of Sadat's references to 'destiny' and its 'decrees', which he sees as shaping his own life from the first.

It is worth trying to trace this political faith, this religious conception of politics, back through Sadat's life and work. Its intellectual origins are apparent in Islamic tradition. But the period of Sadat's intellectual formation in the Egypt of the 'thirties was one in which the political relevance of Islam was being questioned by the young and the intellectually active. It was a period when western influence was strong and when glib western assumptions about the autonomy of politics from religion were popular. Secularism was strong in the Free Officers' Movement, of which Sadat was a founder member. The officers' vision of a strong, modernised Egypt was western-inspired, technologically oriented; it owed little to distinctively Islamic sources and specifically rejected the theocracy of the Muslim Brotherhood.

Yet despite these adverse circumstances the young Sadat began to adumbrate the views which grew into the conception we have described. Two circumstances in the 1940s worked on Sadat's anyway basically religious disposition to produce this effect. There was the consolation of religion during his imprisonment under the British, to which we shall return in a moment. And there was his role as liaison officer between the Free Officers and the Supreme Guide of the Muslim Brotherhood. Sadat, unlike many more susceptible men who met and admired the Supreme Guide, eluded Hassan Banna's spell. The superficiality of the Brotherhood's understanding of the Quran repelled him; the fanaticism worried him; the Supreme Guide's theatricality, his studiously cultivated mystique, his love of gratuitous secrecy, all left Sadat unimpressed. And he was suspicious of Hassan Banna's attempts to use him, to evangelise him, to win him for the

Brotherhood, and through him to absorb the Free Officers into that capacious organisation.

Sadat resisted al-Banna's overtures and insisted on the Free Officers' distinctiveness and independence. But he was not entirely unaffected by his contacts with the Brethren. Hassan Banna's example taught him how Islamic fervour could be compatible with political dynamism and could even be given a revolutionary impulse. Many Free Officers would have agreed with him that the Brotherhood was 'a useful ally to our revolutionary movement', but Sadat went further, regarding militant Islam not only as an ally but as a source of ideology. He felt convinced that 'the dogmas of Islam must be inculcated into all branches of the Army' — an ironic conviction, when we recall how he died.

In fact, the role of the Free Officers in Nasser's time cannot be said to have embodied the Islamic idea of the polity. More recently, however, the effects in Egypt of the religious renaissance that has been felt throughout the Islamic world have brought the popular mood and the tenor of politics in the country more into keeping with Sadat's own religious views. Sadat welcomed the moderate features of this so-called 'Islamic Revolution'. He had an eye to the consistency of the secular law with the Sharia, whilst preserving popular sovereignty with jealous zeal against predatory would-be theocrats; he associated the religious authorities — especially the Shaikh of Al-Azhar (the world centre of Muslim learning in Cairo) — in the process of government, without enslaving the state to the mullahs as has happened in Iran; he reformed some laws in obedience to Quranic precepts, while trying to respect the views of Egypt's large Christian minority; and in other areas of social concern, especially in connection with the penal code and the status of women, he interpreted Islamic tradition broadly in order to accommodate modern needs and demands. In short, he sought to build a genuinely Islamic state, but without any of the intemperate excesses of an Aurangzeb or a Gaddafy.

On the other hand, an Islamic polity is hard to realise in practice, especially in Egypt, where there is a large non-Muslim minority, and in the modern world, where popular expectations are generally governed by secular goals. If Sadat wavered in applying Islam to everyday politics, it was not necessarily because he was 'insincere': on the contrary, the evidence of his own observance, and his own protestations of faith, is consistent and convincing. But circumstances obliged him to compromise. In his early years in power, when he was reacting against most ingredients of Nasserism, including the fiercely secular character of the July Revolution, he felt free to follow his conscience unreservedly. The Islamic renaissance could be encouraged. Militant, fundamentalist Islam could be allowed to organise and express itself. Moderate reforms of law along Islamic lines could be espoused. Events, however, rapidly overtook this policy. Sadat failed to realise that the spirit of militant Islam nurtured in Egyptian universities in the 'seventies was entirely different from — indeed, incompatible with — the conception of an Islamic polity with which he had grown up. It was a spirit that would sanction no state, save a theocracy or a millenial kingdom; it would countenance neither women's rights nor religious tolerance. It anathemised modern society and a modern economy. Moreover, with increasing vehemence from 1974, it spawned violent factions and terrorist cells. Outrages in Egypt, and the daunting examples of unrestrained Islamic militancy of different kinds in Libya, Iran and, to some extent, throughout the Muslim world, forced Sadat to react. Encouragement of Islamic radicals gave way to repression. For the language of a social order based on faith, Sadat began to substitute in his speeches a call for 'a separation of politics from religion'. There is no reason to suppose that Sadat's Islamic ideals had been diluted, but by the end of the 'seventies he was expressing them in language that offended many other Muslims, while comforting secularists. On 15th May, 1980, he summed up his revised attitude in a speech to the People's Assembly, in which he called for further law reforms on Islamic principles but insisted on 'taking religion out of the state' [Al-Ahram, 16th May, 1980]. This was a highly infelicitious formula, which helps to explain the sense of betrayal in which Islamic radicals' hatred of Sadat, by the time of his assassination, was steeped.

To turn from the political to the personal aspects of Sadat's religion: its most conspicuous feature is perhaps its total sufficiency. The president needed no other form of spirituality to enlighten him, therapy to console him, discipline to strengthen him or pleasure to satisfy him than his religion. This made him austere. His austerity was comprehensive. Material possessions and worldly vainglory were, he claimed, without conscious self-deceit, matters of indifference to him. His contempt for personal wealth was a trait he shared with his equally austere predecessors, Saladin, who died with but a few dinars in his coffers, and Nasser, who had only 800 pounds in the bank. It is remarkable that no culumny against Nasser's memory prompted Sadat to a fiercer response than an allegation of pecuniary corruption. The president was also an admirer of Christian asceticism, which he witnessed in Coptic monasteries in his youth and which helped to make him an understanding friend of the Copts and a sympathiser with them in their predicament as a beleaguered minority in Islamic Egypt. He was abstemious in gastronomy, partly out of asceticism and partly out of one of the vanities he permitted himself — concern for his figure. He sadly admitted that he must treat his stomach with caution. His always sensitive digestion was wrecked in prison in the 'forties. Eno's with coffee was his usual breakfast, though he would occasionally add a daring slice of papaya.

That so many of the inescapable rituals of public life are centred on meals of indecent extravagance was a source of boredom and vexation to him. He 'accepted fatigue' as part of his — and Egypt's — way of life [Israeli, 624]; but as far as he could, he tried to concentrate his work into the mornings to allow himself time for physical exercise and for relaxation by watching a film before resuming official engagements. Ironically, the few indulgences this austere man really craved were closed to him — an excursion with his sons, a long walk, a meal out or a visit to the cinema, all these were excluded for reasons of business of state or security. The only taste he could pander to at home was his love of films. Hollywood westerns were his favourite, but their superficial ethics made him restless: he felt the allure of the cowboys' glamour but was attracted to the Indians because they are victims, rather than villains; as a third-world leader, his sympathies were engaged by the oppressed.

Western observers always found it hard to understand how he discharged so much responsibility in the framework of such a leisurely routine. How could he find time not only for an almost daily 'movie' but also for innumerable appearances before the world press and a demanding diurnal round of P.T. and still fit in the duties of an executive president? He was accused of laziness. Modish journalists joked about his 'laid-back' presidential style. Such gibes were ill directed. Sadat's conception of his job was un-western, utterly purged of all phrenesis. He thought a president's role was to think about the major goals of government, to prescribe objectives and to delegate action, not to submerge himself under the numbing waves of day-to-day government business. His style was more like that of a Reagan than a Carter. He filled with reflection and meditation a day which a western executive might fill with action: this was not the result of laziness, but of an alternative approach.

Nasser's attitude had been different: he had tried to do everything and ended by accomplishing little. Sadat's method similarly carried its own dangers and there were areas of governmental activity, particularly of finance, of which he was never fully aware. There were other areas — economic and environmental — where his periodic interventions were often infelicitous because they were ill-informed and under-rehearsed. His successor, Husni Mubarak, has reverted to a more active, even more frantic, routine. But Sadat's style was the only one consistent with his character. Only a contemplative conception of his job could have yielded the great visionary schemes which distinguished his work. To provide the right environment for the peaceful meditation he needed, Sadat and his wife created a chain of presidential 'rest-houses' in quiet parts of the country with inspiring views. Many people found these offensive: they seemed like an ostentatious form of luxury, defacing the landscape. But they were comfortable rather than luxurious, sparsely furnished and moderately equipped — settings for thought, not physical sybaritism, numerous but austere.

The rest-houses excited scandal because they were symbols of presidential aloofness: they insulated Sadat from secular cares. Some western observers identified them with 'conspicuous consumption' and thought they were unpopular in Egypt as evidence of Sadat's links with his capitalist, 'exploitative', middle-class constitutency. That was a travesty of the truth. But Sadat was blamed in Egypt for 'losing touch' towards the end of his life, for turning his politics of withdrawal and detachment into a form of self-indulgence. That was why, when Sadat's successor sent in the bulldozers to obliterate the rest-houses from beauty spots in which they were eyesores, this apparently symbolic reversal of the dead president's 'style' was greeted with general approval.

The charge that Sadat cultivated selective austerity, paradoxically, to the point of self-indulgence has some truth. Asceticism ceases to be asceticism when one wallows in it. But it is only fair to recognise the limits of Sadat's self-denial as human failings, rather than to accuse him of hypocrisy or deceit. He indulged pardonable vanities, apparently without any awareness of the contrast with his eremitical self-image. He loved worldly fame; he took a childish delight in the ephemeral testimonials of pressmen. He kept count of his appearances in the headlines of the world. He liked to be photographed and commissioned the best cameramen to snap him to the best advantage. He was fastidious in his appearance and almost obsessively careful about the contrived simplicity of his clothes. In some degree, Sadat suffered from a peculiarly late twentieth-century *mal de siècle* which politicians share with film-stars and pop-singers and others whose careers depend on the successful marketing by 'the media' of their paper and celluloid images. He became the victim of his own public image, prating about his 'identity' and his 'quest for himself', like an American psychiatrist's client, babbling on the couch. He made the preservation of his own self-awareness more difficult by adopting a political style that emphasised public relations — and, especially, relations with the world's news media. Finally, he had a mystic's typical self-importance, a genuine conviction that he was singled out for a divine 'mission'. It was this conviction that made him relish his own aloofness and the deference of others. None of these failures or quirks made his Islamic faith less thorough-going or his austerity less sincere.

Austerity happens to be relevant to Egypt's general economic problems: it is a prophylactic which, applied on a large scale, could cure the country of corruption and wasteful consumption. It could help to increase investment and exports. But for Sadat it was primarily a private rather than a social virtue. It was a means of personal self-improvement rather than a political slogan. For a man in public life, austerity functions best as a curb on ambition. For years, Sadat surprised his contemporaries with his contentment in minor office. He was self-effacing under Nasser's presidency, even though Sadat's credentials for acclaim as the real founder of the Free Officers and the Revolutionary Movement were unquestionably superior. He never sought an important post, much less the presidency. As he said, 'socially recognisable success' meant little to him [Sadat, 1978, 80]. At times he carried his modesty to excess, like a medieval monk declining a bishopric, as when he accepted the job of Deputy Speaker of the National Assembly in 1957, and evinced reluctance to be Nasser's vice-president in 1969 or to be elected president in 1970. But at least modesty is less of an obstacle to the discharge of duty than ambition.

If Sadat's religion was austere, it was also, like that of so many ascetics, mystical. Mystics often appear egocentric to those who have not shared their experiences, but the sense of assimilation which they feel with God, with a more than individual source of being, often induces the sort of selflessness we see in Sadat's case. 'I regard', he said,

> my last eight months in prison as the happiest period in my life. It was then that I was initiated into that new world of self-abnegation which enabled my soul to merge into all other beings, to establish communion with the Lord of all Being [Sadat, 1978, 85].

Three things combined to make him a mystic: the prison environment, with its strangeness and its strain, conducive to moods of exaltation and new spiritual and intellectual experiments; the deprivation of everyday liberties, inspiring Sadat to seek transcendent forms of freedom through which his mind and soul could escape confinement; and the perusal of writings in the Islamic mystical tradition, for which his imprisonment gave him leisure. Like Al-Ghazzali, he came to mysticism through reading, confirmed by experience. In fact — and it is a fact indicative of Sadat's philosophical eclecticism — the book which triggered the mystical experience he underwent in Cell 54 was neither Sufic nor Islamic, but specifically Christian, *Magnificent Obsession,* by the American pastor and physician Lloyd Douglas. 'In spite of my knowing Quran and learning Quran,' Sadat once said,

> The man who really opened the door of faith for me in Cell 54 is an American author called Lloyd Douglas...This man taught me faith...it was one year and a half before they permitted us to have newspapers and books...Fortunately the first book I read was *Magnificent Obsession* and then continued after that in the same line. In Cell 54, I found myself. I found myself and I found that through love I can

do miracles. Through hatred I am impotent.

But the influence of Lloyd Douglas could only operate through the Islam in which Sadat's thinking was already deeply steeped. Sufism moulded his mysticism. He achieved what he called 'inner light', the awareness of the insignificance of the self compared with humanity, being and God. He found that:

It is only through communion with all existence that a man can really exist. His consciousness can then expand to encompass the entire universe, his individual entity can merge into those of others (by loving them and suffering for them) and, in a word, he ceases to exist in his individual capacity [Sadat, 1978, 81].

There is much of Sufi origin in this: the divine union, the humane conscience, the sense of stages of mystical experience, the emphasis on love. Though there is no evidence that Sadat ever formally became a Sufi initiate, Egypt — a land of 60,000 Sufi confraternities — is rife with the influence of that subtle and numinous discipline, which has long been a refining and ennobling influence on Islam in the area. It was chiefly Sufi scriptures that Sadat read in gaol.

The most suggestive historical parallel for Sadat's relationship with Sufism is again with Saladin, to whom the president often alluded in speeches. Saladin, launching a campaign like Sadat's, eight hundred years ago, to galvanise Egyptian energies and instil Egypt with a sense of mission, found personal inspiration and political relevance in Sufi thought.

Saladin mobilised the Sufis as an educational élite and political vanguard. But, for Sadat, the social relevance of mysticism was more personal, discovered in the social role of love, which gives the individual a sense of responsibility to an ever widening community — first his family, then his nation, then mankind — as his love grows in inclusiveness. It is as though love were a catapult, hurtling inner contemplation into the world and society with tremendous force. Sadat attributed this discovery to the effects of prison life, where his need of love, his starvation of love, made him appreciate love more and deepened his sense of its possibilities: 'My point of departure became love of Egypt, love of all being, love of God' [Sadat, 1978, 87].

This doctrine of the social utility of mystical love is important for the Third World today, which badly needs a vindication of nationalism. Nationalist sentiment is hated in the developed world of western Europe, which has suffered its most destructive effects, its most odious manifestations, yet crucial to the emerging nations, to whom it can impart a sense of unity and purpose. In the light of Sadat's experience and thought, nationalism can be seen to correspond to a phase in the growth and enhancement of love, with the unification of all nations as its natural fulfilment. It may be that the communal way of Sufism was of special significance for Sadat's political thought. His admiration of village communities as model polities reminds us of the mutual help and common worship and meetings or even common life practised by the Sufi orders.

The mysticism Sadat acquired in prison continued to affect him amid the hard realities of public office. He often felt the benefit of periods of retreat or withdrawal for contemplation and meditation: during the 1967 war, for instance, when his only worldly contacts were by telephone with Nasser and Amer; during the impact of defeat, when he shut himself in his home near the pyramids for three weeks; during the weeks before the October war, when the rate of his speeches and public appearances slackened markedly. More importantly, however, his mystical background helped to make him politically active in the effort to realise in practical politics the conception of beauty he achieved through mystical experience. In prison, 'Beauty became my presiding ideal...My idealism a perpetual craving for beauty...inspired by paramount desire to save Egypt from her besetting troubles and to help her advance towards perfection and beauty' [Sadat, 1978, 89].

By 'beauty' Sadat understood whatever conduces to communion, brotherhood, peace between men. One of the sights which most affected him by its 'beauty' in the whole of his career was, for instance, that of Nehru embracing and being embraced by communist deputies in India. Only against the background of the mystical side of Sadat's faith can his love of peace be fully understood. Finally, his mysticism contributed to his equanimity, that most precious of a politician's gifts. During the Yom Kippur offensive against Israel, for instance, Sadat was protected from the phrenesis of war by his utter inner tranquillity: and this in turn enabled him to turn at once, when a constructive victory had been accomplished, to the pursuit of peace.

Faith without charity is of little worth. Loyalty to principles and abstract promises is only lifelessly commendable without loyalty to friends. One of Sadat's most touching qualities was the personal nature of his integrity, his human compassion, the love he learned in gaol through his mystical meditations and spiritual ascent. He revealed the mettle of his friendship to great and small alike — men as small as Ghuwaybah, the war profiteer who gave Sadat sanctuary in his fugitive days of 1944-45 and who, when wealth confiscation measures were introduced in 1961, hid his riches under the floorboards and went round in rags, counting on Sadat's discretion; men as great as the late Shah of Iran, on whom Sadat alone took pity when other former friends deserted him, or Nasser, whose posthumous reputation Sadat spared no effort, short of mendacity, to protect.

Sadat's loyalty to both these fallen Titans of recent history was of one piece. In both cases Sadat's insight separated the private man from his public office. In both cases he spoke of his obligations and relations with the men in terms of love, brotherhood and friendship; in both, he preserved his independence of critical judgement on the nature and shortcomings of their régimes. In both, his loyalty was fired by gratitude. In Nasser's case, one might feel Sadat had little to be grateful for. Nasser had taken over, during his friend's incarceration, the beginnings of a movement that Sadat had effectively founded; he directed it thenceforth, always consulting Sadat but sometimes departing radically from his wishes; he did much, especially once in power, that Sadat disliked; after the accomplishment of the revolution, he entrusted Sadat with largely figurehead roles, carrying little power, such as might have offended a less generous or less ascetic man.

However, Nasser had given his friend something Sadat valued more highly than power or fame: he had won his love during years of close collaboration in the same cause; and he had contributed signally and centrally to the fulfilment of Sadat's dream, the liberation of Egypt [Sadat, 1978, 79]. This enabled them to sustain for eighteen years a harmony that was sometimes disturbed by discords or harsh syncopations, but never disrupted. The vivid, detailed, intimately personal quality of Sadat's appreciation of Nasser came through the appraisal he wrote for his son, who is named after Nasser, in 1958, entitled *My Son, This is Your Uncle Gamal.*

We have already said that this book is full of Sadat's typical undogmatic humanity. It displays an attitude towards Nasser — of friendship transcending differences of opinion — to which he always adhered. Yet the shadow of Nasser grew longer and denser as long as Sadat lived. It was a spectral shadow, which haunted Sadat until he could hardly bear, by the end of his life, to hear his old friend's name mentioned by anyone but himself. Hence the breakdown of his friendship with M. H. Haykal, who was an unremitting reminder of the Nasser years. There was, perhaps, a psychological disturbance of some kind at the root of his relationship with Nasser, whom, revering as a mentor, almost as a father, he resented as one often does resent a father figure. It pained him to have to dismantle Nasser's work and subject his reputation to reassessment. Yet Sadat acknowledged that much of what Nasser did was disastrous for Egypt and had to be changed.

Of Sadat's loyalty towards the Shah of Iran, it is not enough to say that it was of a piece with his loyalty towards Nasser, for the Shah's personal predicament was so much worse. Nasser's suffering after the 1967 débâcle was terrible enough, and Sadat's heart went out to him in grief. But the Shah was a tragic figure of true Aristotelian dimensions. He was neither angel nor saint, but he made himself one of the world's most powerful men and head of one of its most powerful nations by determination and ability. He may have misread his subjects' mood but he never stinted them of his duty or devotion. It is not necessary, to appreciate his tragedy, to say that he was exceptionally good or just, but his fall was not due to wickedness: he was a victim of *hubris* and adverse fortune. The extent of his plunge to a footloose exile and early death was awesome enough. What made it so poignant was the desertion of the friends he made in power. Even President Carter, to whom he had been closest, politically and personally, among his fellow world leaders, reluctantly connived at his discomfiture, granting him no permanent refuge in the United States.

Thus, for Sadat, adherence to their friendship was another matter of 'ethics and principle', like the bond of friendship that made him protect Yusuf Rashad from revolutionary vengeance after 1952. Also, because of the almost universal rejection of the Shah in the Islamic world, it was a matter of religion. Islam enjoins generosity on its adherents, and the Shah had committed no blasphemy, offended no Quranic precept, in his years of power; the worst he had done was to interpret Islam progressively, as Sadat himself also did. In condemning him, fanatics made a travesty of the faith they claimed to uphold. In the circumstances of the Shah's fall, Sadat's conduct was also a matter of common humanity and pity towards a friend in need. Politics were irrelevant: there could be no come-back for the dying, broken man the Shah had become; in befriending him, Sadat was offering no succour to an enemy of the revolutionary régime in Iran. As refuge after refuge closed its doors or was prevented by political imperatives from offering the Shah a berth, as Britain, Morocco, the United States, Panama and the Caribbean states all became inaccessible, as — in short — he was hounded from pillar to post, Sadat hoped, alone among all the leaders of the world, to give him a place to live. As it turned out, all he could be offered was what he was really searching for — a place to die.

Sadat's cordiality towards the Shah had precedents; for instance, it must be remembered, in his 'loving generosity' towards ex-king Idris of Libya, to whom he was in no way beholden. Idris had lived in Cairo, a pathetic figure, since his expulsion from his homeland in 1969, stateless and friendless, till Sadat pityingly allowed him Egyptian nationality. It is also noteworthy that Sadat considerably mitigated the vindictiveness of the Egyptian state towards the Egyptian ex-royal family, to whom he restored some confiscated personal property, judging that they had already lost enough and suffered enough.

Of course, there were bonds of personal sympathy between Anwar El-Sadat and Mohammed Reza Pahlavi. It was for more than mere reasons of political convenience that they spoke of each other in brotherly terms in the days when both were powerful statesmen. They shared some objectives. Both were striving to modernise their countries within limits set by Islamic tradition; both were trying to make free economies work for the public good. Both favoured Islamic and Middle Eastern strength and solidarity. They were both family men, with children of comparable ages and tastes; when state occasions brought them together, they had common human experiences to share. At a deeper level, both were interested in the moral and spiritual forces that motivate nations: that is why both exhorted their people to uphold moral values and traditional virtues. Both were believers in destiny. They shared tastes — a preference for historical reading and a passion for the cinema as a source of relaxation. It would be superficial to say they were similar men. The differences went deeper than the similarities. But their friendship had a broad base.

There are similar points of comparison to be made between Jihan and the Empress Farah and their relationships with their husbands. Both had their husbands' respect and confidence, but neither publicly used her influence to contribute to policy-making, professing the traditional values of the wife as helper and supporter of her husband. Both played leading roles in the emancipation of women in their country. Both have made their mark on questions of broader social welfare. Like Jihan, the empress used to be a glutton for the petitions and complaints of ordinary people; both women became adoptive ombudsmen. Both have worked 'tirelessly' in local or specialised welfare organisations.

Finally, Sadat's relations with the Shah were based on straight-forward gratitude for the solidarity shown with Egypt by the Shah's Iran at the hour of need in 1973. Sadat was pleased with the improvement he had effected in Egyptian-Iranian relations, which had been in ruins when he became president; but it is unlikely that he can have foreseen the crucial role that the countries' new-found friendship was to have in securing Egypt's victory in the October war. The war had to be undertaken at a time when levels of aid from the superpowers were minimal. But Iranian oil aid and arms aid made a decisive difference to Egypt's ability to fight. Sadat could never forget that debt or that it was owed at once to the Iranian people in general and, inescapably, to the Shah in particular.

Of a piece with his loyalty to Nasser and generosity towards the Shah was Sadat's general disposition to tolerance and clemency. Representative of his quality of mercy was his forgiving attitude towards political enemies — enemies as old, for instance, as General Muhammad Naguib, whom he released from seventeen years' detention in 1971; or as dangerous as Shams Badram or Salah Nasr, who benefited from amnesties he conferred; or as numerous as the 12,000 disfranchised victims of the Revolution whose rights he restored in his first months of power. Representative of his tolerance was Sadat's gift of understanding people of other persuasions and other faiths than his own. This was fundamental to his success in rebuilding friendships with long alienated men and nations.

Towards the end of his life, when fear of failure undermined his morale and when the doctrine of toleration was in ruins because of confessional bigotry and rivalry in Egypt, Sadat seemed to discard or suspend his humane principles. He over-reacted to opposition. He abrogated liberties he had personally worked to erect. He imprisoned overt enemies and *fainéant* friends in their hundreds. Perhaps it was just a temporary aberration — an uncharacteristic break with long-standing principles for emergency purposes only. Perhaps, on the other hand, Sadat was in the midst of an irreversible personal and political decline. We shall never know. Sadat was killed in the most inconsistent, self-contradictory phase of his career, before its final direction was revealed.

Faith in Action

After his faith, his fatherland and his family, his peasant origins probably meant most to Sadat. At the opening of his reminiscences he proclaimed himself, 'I, a peasant, born on the banks of the Nile, where man first witnessed the dawn of time.' [Sadat, 1978, 1]. He loved peasant dress and peasant company and the peasant values of neighbourliness and mutual help practised in his home village, where he often returned. What drew him back to his rustic provenance was partly the belief that Egypt, despite industrialisation, remains in a sense a peasant nation, a nation of communities closely enmeshed by ties of reciprocal dependence: his peasant's nature thus brought him close to the heart of Egypt's national identity. Partly, too, it is the peasants' closeness to the sources of existence — land and water and God — that attracted and inspired Sadat. 'The feeling that I am a peasant,' he wrote, 'gives me a rare self-sufficiency' [Sadat, 1978, 42]. He always drew strength from this perception of himself. As a boy, he felt superior to his bourgeois *confrères* at his Cairo school; he fancied he could detect a common closeness to the soil at the root of his good relations with President Carter. 'I find that I am dealing with a man who understands what I want, a man impelled by the power of religious faith — a farmer, like me' [Sadat, 1978, 302].

It is worth noticing that the first words of the president's memoirs refer not only to his peasant background but also to the antiquity of Egypt. These two things were inseparable to Sadat, who wrote:

> Our Egyptian civilisation — which dates back over 7,000 years and is the earliest in human history — has always been inspired by man's love of and attachment to the land [Sadat, 1978, 271].

Sadat was a redoubtable amateur historian: as a schoolboy and cadet he read all the history books he could get. His mind often turned to historical parallels, especially from pharaonic and Islamic history; as we shall often note in the course of the present book, his conception of history influenced his policies time and again. He always loved the study of the subject and tried to persuade his wife to specialise in it at the university. He was perfectly serious about the continuity of Egyptian history, stretching back across the centuries to the time of the pharaohs; and he was quite right, for the ethnic composition of Egypt's population has hardly been tinged by turbulent intervening times. As he told the former American Secretary of State, William Rogers, in 1971, 'You are dealing with a people more than seven thousand years old. Isn't it about time you knew the Egyptian people?' [Sadat, 1978, 281] He stressed continuity not only of identity but also of sense of identity: 'With cultural roots that date back to the fifth millennium B.C. [the Egyptian people] never lose their sense of identity, however hard the circumstances may be' [Sadat, 1978, 204].

The study of history also supplied Sadat with hero figures, men whose example he admired, by whose characters and achievements to set his own standards. For such a self-reliant man, he was remarkably susceptible to the appeal of heroes, perhaps because — and we say this with no desire to deride him — he liked to recognise kindred spirits in them. For a hero is he who stands against the tide of history and, Canute-like, bids it withdraw. The hero resists the impulsion of impersonal historical forces and makes history — or seeks to do so — himself, imposing his individual will and prowess on events that would otherwise be determined by inscrutable and unyielding economic, social, geographical or 'world-historical' factors. Sadat believed in the possibility of heroism so defined. And he tried to realise it in his own life — for instance, in bringing democracy to Egypt when conditions seemed scarcely favourable, and bringing peace when all circumstances seemed adverse.

Of course, this was only Sadat's self-perception. It was not necessarily true, nor necessarily dishonest for being false. It is possible to write the history of Egypt under Sadat's presidency, as Mark Cooper has done, without making the president's personal will appear decisively to influence events at all [Cooper, 1982, *passim*]. Of the great events generally seen as in some special sense Sadat's own work, all can be explained away. The Corrective Revolution of 1971 can be seen as a collective coup by excluded or isolated liberals of whom Sadat was one, followed by the implementation of a programme of liberalisation already announced in Nasser's time. The economic policy of *infitah*, which liberated private enterprise and encouraged western investment, can be seen as an inevitable change which was already under way in the 'sixties or, alternatively, as a political ploy designed to capture a middle-class 'constituency' for Sadat's régime. Sadat's great foreign policy initiatives can be seen as the traditional responses of successive Egyptian régimes to unrest at home. The switch to multi-party democracy on a liberal, western pattern can be seen as willed not by the president but by the increasingly technocratic element in Egypt's gradually but remorselessly changing élite. Sadat himself was probably blind to the influence of these contexts on him. He had a sense of 'a mission in life' for which he thought he had been divinely singled out. If he sometimes saw himself as a labourer in a field, he always saw himself as a meteor in the *néant*. Yet his self-image in this respect overlapped with the truth. He was not the sole progenitor of the Collective Revolution, but it was his skill that brought it off. He was not the sole author of liberalisation, either in the polity or the economy, but his enthusiasm gave it speed and, in some degree, direction. War-mongering and peace-making were not, of course, unprecedented in previous Egyptian history but no one did them quite like Sadat; and while foreign and domestic policies are always inter-dependent (and nowhere more so than in Egypt where foreign affairs are traditionally matters of acute public interest) Sadat always tended to assign priority to foreign affairs by personal taste and, for most of the time, reserved conduct of Egypt's foreign policy to himself. Whatever the relative merits of 'heroic' and 'deterministic' conceptions of history, it is essential, if one is to understand Sadat, to realise that his own conception of it was heroic.

This explains how Sadat could simultaneously embrace in his heart heroes as apparently ill assorted as Gandhi and Napoleon — both figures, like Sadat himself, emblematic of enmity towards Britain but otherwise having nothing in common save dauntlessness in adversity. His short-lived admiration for Hitler can be understood in this context. Napoleon has an extra significance as one of Egypt's modernisers and therefore a historical character to whom Sadat was heir. Gandhi's life had added meaning for Sadat for its devotion to the causes of peace and of the dignity of the emergent, ex-colonial world. His other heroes similarly have special relevance of one sort or another: Saladin, great unifier of the Middle Eastern region against the intrusion of a colonial power; Atatürk, maker of a revolution that was in some ways a pre-enactment of Egypt's own, in a country which had formed part of the same empire, shared similar social and economic problems, inherited much of the same cultural legacy, and possessed, like Egypt, a strategic waterway that invited the cupidity of imperialists; Mustapha Kamil and Muhammad Farid, heroic if unsuccessful leaders in the vanguard of Egyptian nationalism, who 'sought neither position nor wealth' and whom Sadat called on his supporters to imitate.

If there was one quality in Sadat that commanded the respect of friend and foe alike it was his integrity. Everywhere (albeit not by everyone) he was acknowledged to say what he meant with absolute sincerity and to act upon it (though this does not, of course, mean that he never contradicted himself or changed his mind); he was celebrated and sometimes reviled for his loyalty to friends and his fidelity to his promises. Misunderstanding of his basic honesty — which was very real to Sadat, very heartfelt, and a source of proper pride — arose partly from the literal-mindedness of his interlocutors and partly from his inability to 'deliver' all he promised.Sadat was loqacious by nature. By every ordinary standard of loquacity, he talked too much. He loved to 'ad-lib' and to give unscripted interviews. His conversation, especially with press interviewers, if one-sided, was always calculated to communicate charm, as well as more specific messages. He tended to say not only what he wanted to say but also what he thought his audience wanted to hear. This injudicious verbal generosity is almost an Egyptian national vice. It sometimes provokes misunderstandings.

Sadat, for instance, innocently over-committed himself when he promised to make 1971 a 'year of decision'. Even in carefully prepared written statements, he was careless of formal logic, although 'logic' and 'rationality' were always extolled by him and their absence in others deplored. In the renowned *October Paper* of 1974 — the blueprint for all his subsequent policies of liberalisation — he declared himself opposed both to the one-party state and to a plurality of parties, without evincing the faintest awareness of the contradiction. The same sublime indifference to the ordinary disciplines of self-expression came through his unscripted conversations. In the same breath, he told journalists that 'whether I stay on or not depends on the will of God and that of my people...When I feel that I have reached my peak as a creative human being, I will go, whether my people wish it or not' [Müller and Blaisse, 1982, 9]. Yet if Sadat spoke in riddles like the Sphinx and in ambiguities like the oracle of Amun, he genuinely tried to avoid conscious mendacity.

Sadat himself attributed the attainment of honesty to the possession of self-knowledge, for all deceitfulness is in some measure self-deceit. Because he knew himself well enough to try, with variable but remarkable success, to be honest with himself, he could be frank and open with others, even in political relationships where chicanery and staatspolitik were virtually accepted conventions. 'Nothing', he said, is more important than self-knowledge' [Sadat, 1978, 75]. That is why his reminiscences are entitled *In Search of Identity,* a search that began for him when, on first going to Cairo as a small boy, he revelled in his rustic mispronunciation of the word for 'matches', though he was ridiculed for it, because it made him distinctive [Sadat, 1978, 8].

Of course straight talking — 'saying the same thing in private as before the microphones', as Sadat described it [Sadat, 1978, 89] — is something of a luxury and there was a time in his career, during the revolutionary struggle, when he could not afford it. We have seen how he was obliged to show dazzling, almost pyrotechnic, skill in fabrication and equivocation in 1942, when he was under arrest over the affair of the German agents, and managed to bamboozle the British interrogators. He showed the same mastery of deceit after the Amin Osman affair in 1946, when he actually controlled his own interrogation and manipulated those of other prisoners. In 1952, in negotiating with Ali Mahir to preserve continuity of government during the revolution, he deliberately misled the prime minister over the king's fate, suppressing the fact that the Free Officers had already decided for a republic. Even more sadly for Sadat, he had to involve his friend, Yusuf Rashad, who had the king's confidence, in his efforts to encumber the king with misinformation in the period preceding the revolt. He explained it thus:

> Dr Yusuf Rashad was a dear friend whom I had used in misleading the king. Because the issue now at stake was greater than friendship, I refused to talk to him until the battle for the removal of the king was over [Sadat, 1978, 113].

It was only reluctant necessity that compelled him to compromise truth. If he once resorted to that common expedient of revolutionaries — 'the end justifies the means' — he forsook it when the revolution was accomplished and access to power freed him from the need for falsehood. He became the embodiment of his own maxim, 'Some people still believe that politicians say things they don't mean — which I could never do' [Sadat, 1978, 308]. He astonished the world by honouring his promise to go anywhere, even to Jerusalem, in search of peace in 1977; but it was the same world that had not got to know the Egyptian people in 7,000 years and had not yet got to know Sadat.

Many of Sadat's character traits seemed ill adapted to politics. Mysticism, faithful adherence to awkward promises, unflinching loyalties to luckless friends — these are not typical items of a politician's professional equipment. But Sadat contrived to be a man of principle and pragmatism simultaneously. He was never afraid to adopt a policy because of its practical utility rather than because of its compliance with entrenched positions, received dogmas, or unpractical prejudices. For instance, he was a socialist but was unawed by socialist shibboleths: he halted further nationalisation within two months of his assumption of the presidency because he realised that individual enterprise had to be encouraged in order to make the Egyptian economy work. He traversed the terrible taboos that impeded peace with Israel. He rejected the doctrinaire pan-Arabism of the Gaddafy camp in favour of a realistic, gradualistic approach to Arab unification. He stood outside the excesses of Islamic revolutionary fundamentalism and tried instead to reconcile Islamic traditions with the exigencies of the modern world.

The Arabs are not renowned in the western world for pragmatism: the western stereotype is of unrealistic romantics, imagining six impossible things before breakfast. But Sadat did not accept this image. He even called pragmatism 'Arab logic', pointing out that in the post-war years the Arabs — or, at least, the Egyptians — expected the Americans to see the sense of conciliating oil-rich states rather than antagonising them by too close an alignment with Israel [Sadat, 1957, 88]. Above all, he stressed the 'objectivity' and realism of his own peace policy: he knew that since America's special relationship with Israel could not be terminated it would have to be accommodated, and that since Egypt could no longer afford war she must make peace. Despite his confidence in 'Arab logic', Sadat's realism won little praise in the Arab world. But realism possesses the quality of vanquishing its opponents in time by the sheer irresistibility of its impetus. The rapprochement between Egypt and the moderate Arab states is already well advanced — incubating under the shell of adverse rhetoric.

Finally, Sadat's pragmatism showed through in the way he applied his own experience in his statecraft. He was an empirical politician. For example, it was his own revulsion from the conditions he endured in the Central Prison that decided him to order a programme of prison rebuilding in the 'seventies. In restoring the rule of law to Egypt after twenty years' suspension, he was applying a lesson he learned under the British, who, whatever the defects of their régime in Egypt, had at least always respected the rule of law — allowing Sadat, for instance, to vindicate himself (albeit falsely) over the Amin Osman affair.

Sadat's faith can be seen at work in his family life and particularly in his relationship with his wife, who had a faith of a similar quality and depth. Jihan is a woman in whom the traditional and the unconventional are nicely blended; but her background is very different from her husband's: her origins are *petit bourgeois*. Her father met his English bride while studying in England. Her mother, Gladys Cottrell, made an audacious marriage. She had to forsake a home and way of life she loved for an unknown land and future that filled her with foreboding. She had to embrace the unaccustomed disciplines of the Islamic religion and the challenging vocation of a Muslim wife. Her reaction to her unexpected destiny tells us much about her own character and, by inference, much about her daughter. She accepted Islam wholeheartedly, yet without effacing her own strong personality. She created a home life for her husband and children in which love and discipline both abided, but 'love was pre-eminent'. Her husband responded warmly and generously, ranking his children equal in love and showing no special favour to the boys over the girls.

To the love of England, which she never lost, Gladys added an equally sincere and arguably more tender love for her adopted country; she passed her love of Egypt on to her children and encouraged them to be nationalists, even — in the conditions of the 1940s — at the cost of being anti-British. Her sensitivity to the mood of nationalism among the Egyptians who surrounded her, even — nay, especially — in the bosom of her own family, is the more remarkable because she never adapted to some of the superficial aspects of Egyptian life: she never liked Egyptian food, but shared the desperate gastronomic chauvinism so typical of the English expatriate; she retained her characteristically English middle-class colour prejudice. Yet, under the shell of these appearances, her depth of feeling for Egypt incubated. Her acculturation was thoroughgoing. And under her wing an uncompromisingly Egyptian family grew up.

Jihan, like her future husband, was lucky to be able to supplement her Muslim home life with a period in a Christian school, though she offended the school establishment by her unwillingness to attend church services, and her parents had to make it clear that these scruples must be respected. Her interest and proficiency in English and history showed how she took after her mother and would be useful later when her formal education was resumed. But for the time being her marriage to Anwar Sadat interrupted her studies. She was only fifteen when they met and the romantic appeal of the young revolutionary, who was poor and footloose only because he was dedicated to the struggle for Egypt's liberation, swept her off her feet. 'I respected Anwar Sadat because he was so dedicated — this', she has said, 'is the main thing that attracted me. He wasn't a rich man, he wasn't good-looking, he wasn't from a very high family. It was his personality' [Quoted by Gloria Emerson in *Vogue*, January 1980, p.203]. She fell in love with him while eating a mango after a day's fasting in Ramadan: these were perfect circumstances — the Islamic symbolism of Ramadan, the ascetic preparation of the fast, the exalted mood of the season, the romantic flavour of the mango, and the adventure of falling in love, all struck what were to be keynotes of her future life as

Sadat's wife. The setting was the house of her cousin, Hassan Izzat, Sadat's friend and fellow revolutionary. Young as she was, Jihan could already sense and share the nationalist fervour of her fiancé. Ironically, in her Anglophile household, she had been brought up to it. 'My mother had such great spirit,' she has said, 'she taught me to love my country' [Ibid]. The nationalist struggle, as well as Sadat's personal qualities, attracted her. 'One of the things I married my husband for,' she once revealed, 'was politics'.

For eighteen years she led as conventional a life as possible in the circumstances of exception and emergency that surrounded the Free Officers' revolution and the early years of the Egyptian republic. She stayed at home, cared for the children, went out rarely in public, had no career of her own, and was more a spectator than a participant in her husband's. But by the late 'sixties all her children had outgrown infancy and she felt called by the urgent circumstances of war and suffering to desert the sidelines and enter the thick of the mêlée. Egypt was crying out for the efforts and sacrifices of all her people, men and women alike without discrimination, to take a share of the national burden and play a part in the national struggle. It was the 1967 war, and the suffering of the wounded soldiers, that impelled her to act. She joined the Red Crescent and was among the first women to go to the front to minister to the victims of the fighting. Her vision of the horrors of war changed her view of her own life. She began to deny little forms of indulgence to her children out of respect for the miseries of the sufferers and to create a sense of dedication and service to others, in imitation of her husband, in the Sadat household.

The 1967 war had a similar effect on Egyptian women to that of the First World War on the womanhood of Europe. It left women like Jihan Sadat with a conviction of their abilities and a taste for responsibility. When her husband came to power, she sought a distinctive role and, in imitation, perhaps, of him, a distinctive public image. The result was a flurry of activity in every conceivable charitable direction, an alignment with progressive and secular causes on social issues and, above all, a commitment to the international 'women's movement'. This was not entirely helpful to her husband. It cut across the currents of Islamic revivalism that were gaining strength in Egypt. But Jihan was a fervent devotee of the 'Super-woman' cult, projecting herself as simultaneously a career-girl, a road-soiled campaigner, and a model wife and mother. The constituency she courted was largely foreign. She claimed to adopt her role as a feminist heroine out of the sort of pragmatism that characterises her. It was Egypt's need to supplement manpower with womanpower in the war-fraught and difficult period at which her husband came to power that made her take a lead in the emancipation and mobilisation of Egyptian women. As a deeply convinced Muslim, living within a profoundly Islamic country, Jihan had to develop her work for women within Islamic traditions. She enthusiastically embraced Islamic constraints. But she found in those traditions a way of life and thought entirely sympathetic to her own views and entirely satisfactory to most women's proper aspirations. As she told the International Women's Conference in México in 1975, in what has become one of her most famous speeches:

> It is the basic tenets of Islam which have always animated our attitude towards the problems of our sex...From the earliest times Islamic society has been one in which women have enjoyed complete economic and social equality with men, and it is only under foreign domination that attitudes, profoundly alien to Islamic thinking, were allowed to creep into the fabric of society.

Indeed, Muhammad's view of women's place in society was, by any standards, enlightened for its day, and Jihan's efforts to transmute Quranic precept, without altering its substance, into twentieth-century terms, have the support of the overwhelming weight of juridical and theological opinion among the Egyptian establishment.

Jihan's is an essentially moderate feminism, exemplified in her own life of uncritical support for her huband. She practises the feminism of partnership, cooperation, and love between the sexes. She has summarised it in a message to the Women's International League for Peace and Freedom:

> It is extremely important that we direct our energies where they would be most useful; not waste them in hysterical cries for revolutionizing and, in the process, jeopardizing the man—woman relationship. It is important to realize and to prove to all that we are partners, not competitors, in the struggle for a better world. That we complement, not contradict, one another. That is best done by discovering our

true realm and functioning wholeheartedly within it, with the sincere conviction that each grain of energy exerted, each little result achieved, contributes to the whole.

These words are virtually a characterisation, in generalised terms, of her own marriage. She denounces the excesses of western feminism, with its brashness, its aggression, its abrasiveness. Thus, for example, she upholds modesty of dress but rejects the use of the veil, declaring her belief in 'a deeper Islam than that'. She used to hold meetings at universities to discourage students from a form of dress which, she believes, is only mistakenly associated with Islam.

Consistent not only with the principles of Egyptian religion, Jihan also claimed that her feminism is part of the traditions of Egyptian nationalism. The interlocking of the causes of female emancipation and national liberation goes back to the time of Tahtawi and Qasim Amin. It was upheld by the Free Officers' Movement: the National Charter and Constitution, for instance, proclaimed by the revolutionaries of 1952, promised equality for women 'without violation of Islamic law'. Yet it must be acknowledged that the revolution achieved relatively little for women until Jihan Sadat came to the fore. The change in style was apparent as soon as she entered the presidential residence, walking alongside her husband, appearing with him on official occasions, and even appearing in public in her own right — something Mrs. Nasser had never ventured to do. In 1975 she headed the all-female Egyptian delegation to tour African and Arab countries in support of the United Nations International Women's Year. The following year she made a similar pilgrimage to the Far East, identifying with women throughout the Third World.

In fact, in the Sadat marriage, Jihan was the more dynamic partner. Sadat could be galvanised into tremendous activity, but only by fits and starts. His style was contemplative rather than active. He would dream and meditate and have visions; he would delegate; only at intervals, after long preparation, would he act. His widow is a woman of action, who plunged into her work with an enthusiasm akin to frenzy.

The energy required to sustain such an active life in the interstices of her researches into Shelley's influence on Arabic literature and her teaching duties at Cairo University is perhaps a clue to the bonds of common interest that united her to her husband. Sharing considerable intellectual prowess and physical energy, they could remain a closely united couple — and the heart of a closely united family — even amid the enormous responsibilities and divers tasks with which they were surrounded. Though Eyptian feminists regarded her as a leader — 'someone to pull us together, to inspire us, to work for our common good', as Amini Al-Said has said — Jihan aimed to be a complement to her husband, a help and support to him, not a politician in her own right. She never tried to influence policy except in uncontroversial areas of social concern.

Only by calling publicly for legislation favouring contraception, which the president regarded as an area to be left to private conscience, has she contributed in any sense to what has been in effect a political debate — and even here the social implications are paramount. 'For political matters', she once said, 'I must try to give my husband the peace and silence he needs to think and work. Sometimes he asks my opinion, but that does not mean he takes my advice. He does not need advice. He is a leader.' Even in the cause which is perhaps closest to her heart as a woman and a mother, the cause of peace, she resisted the temptation to lobby her husband. She has spoken and written in praise of peace to a wider audience. She supported her husband's efforts at home. She showed that she shared his magnanimity and generosity towards the foe in her poignant correspondence with Israeli wives and mothers of war victims. But she did not try to coerce or cajole her husband into a policy of peace. Sadat, as in so much else was naturally in sympathy with her in this. Viewed from one aspect, their joint championship of peace was a projection of their family life onto a bigger screen and scale.

Jihan was an essential part of her husband's success. It is difficult to imagine Sadat without her. Equally, towards the end of his life, when her own overstretched energies were flagging, it became apparent that she also depended on him. She reacted to his death with outward stoicism and inner prostration. Grief broke through her guard in public only in tears shed at the funeral, at the moment of the lowering of the coffin. After the burial, she shut herself away in a kind of self-immolation, as though drained of the drive she had shown for so long. For her tremendous efforts, her staggering rate of activity, had been called forth by the needs of her husband's career.

Of course, integrity and energy — the defining qualities of the public images respectively of Sadat and his wife — are both expendable virtues. No politician of integrity can survive without some power of self-dissimulation. No sincerity can cope with undiluted truth. Like Henry VIII, Sadat can be praised for deceiving others only where he had first deceived himself. This characteristic never became dominant, but it did grow as time went on. When, towards the end of his life, his satisfaction with his own moral standards became saturated, he slipped his guard. His confidence in the purity of his motives emboldened him to step outside his code and submit to petulance and vindictiveness. In a similar way, Jihan's energy became increasingly self-obsessed — diverted, that is to say, into sustaining the image as much as the reality of constant philanthropic activity. The need to court world public opinion absorbed all too much time. Jihan was beginning to tire of the strain of public life — though she loved its exhilaration and its rewards — and seemed driven to cope with desperate recklessness and diminishing returns until, on her husband's death, she virtually collapsed. And, with a healthy feminine liking for adulation, she encumbered her husband's entourage with courtiers whose aims were not always as selfless as the presidential couple's. In these ways, Sadat and his wife exposed their reputations and character to criticism — not to say calumny — which has become so strident and disproportionate that the balance now needs to be redressed. Sadat longed for the heroic stature he once criticised Nasser for seeking. If he fell short of his superhuman ideal, it was in pardonably human ways.

CHAPTER FOUR

Years of Achievement at Home

The Revival of Egypt's National Spirit

Sadat called his fellow Egyptians "a people who are working for a modern civilisation comparable to the one they erected thousands of years ago in freedom and peace" [Sadat, 1978, 313]. Many of the problems which have surrounded or impeded the revival of Egypt's national spirit in the twentieth century are implicit in those words: the conviction that a sense of continuity with the great ancient past is essential; the feeling that Egypt has declined relatively to newer powers; the opinion that part of the key to revival lies in 'modernity' — that is, in emulating the scientific, technical and industrial achievements of the countries that have come to play in the modern world the same sort of leading role that Egypt enjoyed in antiquity; the belief that individual liberty and peace for the country as a whole are prerequisites for the attainment of these goals. Each of these themes exercised Sadat's efforts: in connection with each, he helped the Egyptian people to progress. In consequence, in the great central period of his presidency, when his success was at its height, from 1973 to 1977, Egypt seemed to be experiencing a national rebirth. Her people were finding their ancient virtues again, like the Chinese of the Ming Revolution or the Italians of the Renaissance.

Prompting the people's memory, Sadat evoked the ancient civilisation by frequent allusions to it and by a search to realise parallels with the past. In 1976, for instance, recalling the Pharaohs Thut-Moses I and Thut-Moses III, and alluding at the same time to the war of 1973, he reminded audiences that "when the primitive Hyksos tribes invaded Egypt, the Egyptian will-power ultimately overpowered and expelled them, together with the Hebrews" [Israeli, 1336]. In that reference to 'Egyptian will-power' lies an appeal for a revival of national spirit. It is worth observing that Sadat was also alert to more recent historical parallels: Saladin, in particular — whose eight hundred years of antiquity seem little in comparison with the æons of the pharaohs — was a favourite character of his. In 1971, especially, the president's speeches were prolific in references to him: the great Sultan's gift for inspiring unity was appropriate in the year of Sadat's Corrective Revolution and purge of Ali Sabry's pro-Soviet clique. But the pharaohs are of greater worth as a source or reference, not only because of the splendour and superiority of ancient Egypt, but also because they serve as vivid reminders of the great length of the history of Egyptian national identity. As Sadat put it:

> Egyptian society should go back to its genuine values, which have maintained its unity and distinctive character down the centuries and enabled it to conquer all invaders [Sadat, 1978, 81].

Sadat's revival of the name of Egypt in the official designation of the country emblemised his concern for a distinctly Egyptian nationalism. It is significant, of course, that the name of 'Egyptian Arab Republic' has replaced that of 'United Arab Republic' — significant of Egyptian weariness, at the end of the Nasser years, with vague imperial dreams of pan-Arabism which had brought no successful experiments in unification of Arab countries and which threatened Egyptian identity. The problem in recent years has been to find a form of national self-expression for Egypt without disloyalty to Arab fraternity and solidarity. The solution Sadat endeavoured to inculcate has been well summarised recently by M. B. Ghali:

> The meaning of our national identity thus becomes clear: no idea of race, but an ethnic character made up of human elements that have been blended into a well defined nation; no religion asserting its superiority over others, but a religious character deeply inspired by the principles common to the monotheistic religions; no culture wavering between the different contributions to the Egyptian heritage, but a national culture which embodies them all in a living synthesis; no negative conservatism, no timorous retreat, but an opening onto the West as onto the East and then onto everything that is human in the widest and most generous

sense; no hesitation between the Egyptian nation and the Arab community, but an Egyptian people conscious of their particular identity as well as of the fact of belonging to the Arab community [Ghali, 1978, 32].

The clarity of such a picture was obscured in Nasser's time by hostility to the western world — precluding Egyptians from continuing their historic role as mediators between the occidental and Arabic civilisations — and by obsessions with pan-Arabism. Sadat contrived a more judicious mixture of the elements of Egyptian history.

In fact, it is doubtful whether Sadat was ever an 'Arab nationalist' in the strict sense of the term. He was an Egyptian nationalist, bred in childhood in awareness of the Egyptian community and hatred of the British imperial mastery that muffled its tentative self-expressions. He regarded the Arabs not as a nation but as a group of peoples with allied interests — interests shared in part with the non-Arab peoples of the Middle East. The special role he conceived for Egypt as leader — cultural mouthpiece, technological showpiece, and demographic giant — of the Arab world made particular sense in the Arab context, because of the community of language and religion that embraces all the Arabs. But it made just as much sense in a wider setting too.

Sadat's most cherished vision for the Middle East was of a kind of regional Common Market, which would include Israel and the Christian communities within the Arab states in partnership with the Arab peoples. He was deeply impressed by the way Europe had been transformed from cockpit to community by the E.E.C. He had seen too many ramshackle integration projects collapse in his own region — the U.A.R., the F.A.R., the madcap Gaddafy schemes for instant symbiosis — to believe in any but the most gentle and long-term means to such an end, founded on an economic basis, which most recent schemes have lacked. This was arguably one of the most constructive of Sadat's visions, but also the most offensive to entrenched prejudices and the least likely to survive him.

The drive for 'modernisation' as part of Egypt's revival — for scientific and technical up-dating — depends closely on Sadat's *infitah* or opening to the west. Modernisation does not mean uncritical westernisation — that would be unthinkable in an Islamic country.

Sadat's projected 'leap to the new state' meant, he said, that 'we shall build the Modern State by means of science and technology, and all the achievements of the 20th century, as well as by Faith' [Israeli, 87]. There was a social dimension to this: Sadat also talked of getting Egypt 'out of the Middle Ages', turning it 'from a semi-feudal society into a modern, ordered, viable state' [Sadat, 1957, 53]; but, especially since the land reforms initiated by the July Revolution, there has been little utility in the term 'feudalism' for Egypt, which more resembles a yeoman society or the peasant society of post-revolutionary France than a properly feudal one.

Modernisation is more pertinent — as we shall see — in harnessing scientific progress for social welfare, bringing medical advances to the countryside, emancipating socially disadvantaged groups like women and religious minorities, and improving the efficiency of the administration and public sector industries. Of crucial concern to Sadat were the limits of modernisation. Even in the headstrong revolutionary days of the 'fifties he was vigilant for the conservation of the traditional values he loved so deeply, valiant in the fight to hold the frontier between revolution and destruction. He was for 'respecting the customs of the people... not chaining them to a dead past [but]...respecting the essential and invisible communities in a nation's life. We would conserve everything that did not impede the real progress of the community' [Sadat, 1957, 53].

'Invisible communities' is a good phrase for the sources of co-operation which have always made Egyptian society remarkably cohesive. For most of the country's history, irrigation has been the spur, compelling neighbours to mutual help. There is probably no irrigation problem in the world so productive of reciprocity among neighbours as that of the Nile valley, because the season of the floods is so brief and the labour so urgent and intensive. The basic irrigation community is the village, and Sadat, himself a product of village life, perceived how the villagers' sense of mutual belonging must form the nucleus of any genuinely Egyptian national identity. That is why he 'tirelessly advocated the adoption of the values of the village' [Sadat, 1978, 83].

The vital element of mutual co-operation makes an Egyptian village like a big family, where 'the people are one': according to

Sadat, Egypt as a nation should have the virtues of a family or a village [*Arab Report*, 31st May 1971]. Ironically, since the July revolution, the village communities have shrunk and the numbers of peasants have declined, as migrants have been attracted to the towns by increasing industrial activity. Only half of Egypt's work-force is now employed on the land. But, for Sadat, the countryside remained the essential Egypt. 'Cities', he said, 'do not faithfully reflect our people, only villages do...Since time immemorial, the village has reflected a true picture of our people, that is one family' [Israeli, 263]. In the villages, co-operation amounts to sharing — shared work, shared implements, shared lives — and so mutual dependence and intimate mutual knowledge. Sadat's words again provide the best insight:

> Egyptian will-power is a collective one, not the monopoly of one person or one group. Let us go to the village and see for ourselves. Do you think that each village has its own agricultural implements, such as ploughs and threshing-sledges and irrigation facilities? Do you think that every peasant owns such instruments? Certainly not. These implements are scarce. But a collective will is there, which makes the peasants take turns in using the plough and the threshing-sledge. They thereby function as one family in our society [Israeli, 1343].

Egyptians tend to trace the recovery of their national identity from the October War of 1973. For Tawfik al-Hakim, for instance, and there could be no more representative voice, the war marked 'a spiritual crossing to a new stage in our history...the reconstruction of our civilisation' [*Al-Ahram*, 7th Dec 1973]. And it is true that even authentically historical nationalism, nurtured over hundred of years, needs challenges and triumphs to sustain it and make it grow. Between 1967 and 1973 the Egyptians felt they were stagnating in a position of submission enforced by the super-powers; national dignity demanded that they break out of the impasse, even if only for the sake of their own self-respect. By crossing the Suez Canal to attack the Israelis, they traversed a psychological obstacle as well as a military one. But a revolution in national consciousness cannot be wrought at a stroke. The October war was only part of a process. It had to be followed up with political initiatives designed to allow the Egyptians' renascent sense of nationhood to develop and their newly liberated energies to work.

One part of the process can be glimpsed in the 'era of peace' proclaimed in Egypt in 1979 on the eve of the sixth anniversary of the October war, when the new government of Mustapha Khalil pledged itself to eliminate from the administration the corruption, inefficiency, indiscipline, and neglect that stifled the national spirit. In the same connection, Sadat coined the phrase 'October generation' to denote the young people who took part in the war or whose earliest active memories date from that glorious and optimistic period, unencumbered by recollections of worse times further back.

Another area in which popular energies have had to be liberated in order to complete the mobilisation of Egypt's national spirit is the economy. Sadat explained how, in Nasser's time, the socialism of the government had become tinged with Marxism: 'individual effort came to a standstill and from this stemmed the terrible passivity of the people' [Sadat, 1978, 213]. We shall see how Sadat's economic policy cohered with his efforts to stimulate an Egyptian national revival in due course. The last set of constraints from which the national spirit has had to be freed is political: as an American scholar has perceptively written:

> Egyptians working in all spheres have found themselves trapped, like the characters in Aly Salim's play [*The Buffet*, 1968, in which the protagonist's creativity is stultified by other characters who can be taken to represent authority and bureaucracy], in a network of repressive social structures, their creative energies and generosity of spirit dissipated and subverted [Baker, 1978, 173].

Sadat toiled to put this right. The story of his achievements in this connection is the story of the introduction of democracy to Egypt. Naturally, it was limited democracy, subject to periodic interference and partial abrogation, easily ridiculed by counsellors of perfection. But it is the positive aspects that concern us here. The points to remember are not that Sadat's system was wanting in democracy by British or American standards, but that it was much less authoritarian than Nasser's, much more democratic than the African or Arab norm. To a great extent it was Sadat's own handiwork, and while it is not beyond criticism it deserves respect.

The Introduction of Democracy

> Freedom is the most beautiful, holy and precious fruit of our
> culture; an individual should never be made to feel that he is
> at the mercy of any force or coercion or that his will is sub-
> jected to that of others [Sadat, 1978, 78].

These words of President Sadat's, with their powerful
commitment to political democracy and a degree, at least, of economic
liberation, express one of the most signficant themes of his years in
office. But even as a democrat, Sadat was never doctrinaire. In the
early days of the Free Officers' rule, his first disagreement with Nasser
showed them in what since then have come to seem unwonted — even
reversed — roles, with Nasser arguing strongly to conserve elements
of democracy inherited from the monarchy, Sadat pronouncing for
their suspension in favour of a period of emergency, dicatorial rule,
because 'I was certain that the people had lost faith in the existing
democratic system'. Nasser prophesied danger and bloodshed in the
event of dictatorship and pressed his dissent to the point of
resignation. But his colleagues prevailed. He accepted reinstatement.
A period virtually bereft of democratic institutions ensued.

The subsequent history of Nasser's régime tempts one to feel that
perhaps in his early democratic avowals he protested too much; but
that would be unjust. Rather, Nasser always had a democratic ideal in
his mind and sometimes to the fore of it. But he never had the
opportunity or the capability to achieve it amid the practical realities of
ruling Egypt. I intend to suggest that like many of his subjects Nasser
was a prisoner of the limitations of the system over which he presided;
only his successor had the courage and detachment to break that
system and introduce genuine democracy to Egypt. We must begin by
trying to understand the nature of Nasser's régime, for this was the
starting-point from which democracy struggled for utterance and
Sadat strove to give it speech.

Nasser had already begun the drift to dictatorship, even before his
colleagues had pronounced in its favour: on July 27th, 1952, he
insisted that the Constituent Council of the revolution change its
name to the Revolutionary Command Council. But the autocratic side
of the régime soon came to prevail over these auguries of collective
dictatorship. Sadat said that Nasser 'concentrated all power in his own

hands' [Sadat, 1978, 138], but in practice, of course, autocracy was more limited than that: it was an autocracy in conception, a more complex and less readily definable type of state in execution. Like all tyrants, Nasser was unable to monopolise the sources of power, although the effort to do so helped to consign him to an early grave. Like all tyrannies, his rule spawned intermediate layers of authority, a sort of black market in power which he was unable to control.

Nasser was personally incorruptible, but the corruption which always feeds on power was nourished instead in the persons of his subordinates. In the cabinet, in the administration and bureaucracy, in the ruling party and its secret 'Vanguard', in the organs of justice and enforcement, in the army and above all in Nasser's entourage, groups emerged who diverted patronage, wealth and the means of inflicting pains and punishments from the state. This monstrous usurpation, this grand-scale *lèse majesté*, was unaffected by constitutional sanctions (for there was no full or permanent constitution), unbalanced by the rivalry of legitimate sources of authority (for there were none, save the overworked Nasser himself), untempered by democratic opposition or press scrutiny (for none was permitted), ungoverned by institutions of state (for these were few, rudimentary, and vulnerable to manipulation by the power-croppers). In some ways the power of men like Amer and Sabry ominously recalled the days of the pashas. Nasser was like one of the sultans of old, cocooned in a seraglio of intrigue, while the pashas exploited his subjects for gain.

Sadat well understood the nature of his predesssor's régime. Looking back on the 'sixties in June 1977, he said that the experiment in socialism failed partly because 'it culminated in the rise of centres of power like the Pashas of the pre-revolutionary era' [*Arab Report*, 30th June 1977]. More recently he wrote:

> I believe that a one-man rule is fraught with dangers. Because no one man can really know everything, some of his assistants will...run amuck — creating power blocs, just as happened in Nasser's case [Sadat, 1978, 206].

He believed that Nasser erred in valuing power above love, benevolence and beauty, repressing the sovereignty of the individual, for — in Sadat's judgement — Egyptians' nature was strongly individualistic and therefore alien from such an approach.

Yet, if power centres and the repression of liberty were two aspects of the system which he was resolved to dispel, there were other 'exaggerated and exceptional measures' (as he has euphemistically called them) of the Nasser years which he found even more distasteful. As early as February 1973 Sadat was recalling the 'sixties with disarming frankness in briefings to the information and press community, denouncing the 'Kingdom of Salah Nasr', the sadistic, torturing chief of Nasser's intelligence service.

In some ways, the intelligence service was one of the most dangerous 'power centres' of the sixties; to bring it under control and emasculate the threat it posed to the liberties of citizens was among Sadat's first acts as president. On his first day of office he ordered all telephone-tapping to be discontinued; in May 1971 he ordered the burning of all secret tapes, the closure of detention centres, and the end of arbitrary arrests. But it was only gradually that the truth about the tortures became generally known. Disclosures reached a climax in 1975-76, with a court award in April 1975 against the secret police in favour of Ali Graisha who had been tortured under interrogation ten years earlier; in June 1976 followed the conviction of Salah Nasr himself for use of torture. Meanwhile, a film based on a novel by Naguib Mahfouz, portraying the truth about the secret police under the previous régime, was playing to packed houses all over Egypt. The secret police had been a poisonous offshoot, sprung from a rotten system. But, in trying to reform it when he came to power in 1970, Sadat had to contend with the usurped strength of the neo-pashas.

The need for a new system, based on democratic institutions which would make the 'power centres' wither, was well expressed within a few weeks of Nasser's death by M. H. Haykal in words which closely reflected Sadat's own thinking: 'Nasser was the symbol of the people's authority. After his departure, the authority of the people can only be guaranteed by constitutional and legal safeguards' [*Al Ahram*, 6th November, 1970]. This was delicately put, since a glaring need for such safeguards had already existed while Nasser was still alive. But the import of the message was clear. The 'centres of power' had to be replaced with what Sadat would come to call the 'state of institutions'.

The vital stage in Sadat's show-down with the old system came in 1971; its crucial month was May, to which Sadat ascribed what he called the 'Corrective Revolution' — corrective, that is, of the course of the July Revolution which had brought the Free Officers to government but which had since gone awry with the excesses of the 'sixties and had failed to make progress towards democratic goals. The events of May 1971 came about because a *vieille garde* opposed Sadat's plan to introduce a 'state of institutions': that at least was the underlying cause; but at the time the trigger events seemed to be the negotiations Sadat was pursing for a federation with neighbouring states and the conspiratorial activities of Ali Sabry.

In November 1970, conscious of Nasser's mantle and of the importance of continuity in Egyptian policy, Sadat had signed the Tripoli Charter — a basis of future federation between Egypt, Libya and Sudan; while Sudan had not been party to further steps towards federation, Syria had joined the new 'Federation of Arab Republics' and a common policy-making body had been set up, though the institutional framework of the federation was very sketchy. Ali Sabry was said to oppose the federation plans and it is certainly true that he wanted a more leftist (not to say communist) Egypt than would have been possible in close association with anti-communist neighbours. Sabry had already shown himself too gross a Marxist for Nasser's taste. He had been dismissed from the post of Secretary-General of the Arab Socialist Union in September 1969, after a visit to Moscow, yet so great were his power and influence, and so strident the claims of the left wing, that Sadat had felt willing to make him a vice-president and restore him to some of his A.S.U. posts. His attempts to obstruct the Federation of Arab Republics were conducted more or less openly, as was his opposition to Sadat's peace initiative of 1971 and declaration of willingness to reopen the Suez Canal.

On May 2nd, two days before the American Secretary of State, William Rodgers, was due to arrive for talks, Sabry was dismissed: in the circumstances, a Muscovy duck, cackling after Russian masters, would have embarrassed the government. Sabry's departure cast no ripple of support for him or opposition to the president in popular or political waters. He responded by turning from opposition to clandestine subversion. It will be many years before the real nature and objectives of the conspiracy are known. The chief conspirators were Sabry, Muhammed Fayik (minister of information), Abul Nir (secretary of the A.S.U. Central Committee), Labib Shukair (speaker of the People's Assembly — Sadat's own old job), Sharawi Gomaa (minister of the interior) and the minister of defence, Mahmud Fawzi, who had long been a close political associate of Sadat's but had apparently been lured into the malcontents' camp by a promise of the role of head of state. In addition there was a sort of conspiratorial penumbra in the bureaucracy, composed of the clients and dependents of this coterie: in all, ninety-one officials were to be condemned for participation in the plot.

Even in the course of the trial, the conspirators' objectives remained obscure: some were intent upon a *coup;* others seem to have seen themselves as a militant ginger group, aiming to take power gradually or to build up a controlling interest, rather than a monopoly, in the power of the state. It was on May 1st that Sadat uttered what was in effect a challenge to the malcontents in calling for a 'codification of the Revolution' and a permanent written constitution. Over the next ten days, the conspirators committed desperate indiscretions. An army officer loyal to Sadat was able to bring him incriminating tapes of conspiratorial meetings, in which references were made to a plan to take over Cairo radio station and an aborted plot to seize the president. The threat had to be met decisively. On May 13-15th, Sadat carried out what was almost, in effect, a counter-coup against the malcontents. Most of the leading conspirators resigned their posts on the 13th; expulsions from the People's Assembly followed on the 14th; the non-parliamentarian officials implicated in the plot resigned on the 15th.

Inasmuch as they were intended as a coup, the plans of Sabry and his friends were botched and ineffective. General Fawzi was supposed to pressurise the Central Committee of the A.S.U. into support for Sabry by ordering menacing troop movements; but the soldiers were unwilling to be used as stooges: it was obvious from a meeting of military leaders Sadat had called on the night of April 21st that almost the entire army leadership was in support of the legitimate government. And Fawzi, in the event, lacked the guts to order any troop movements of an unambiguously provocative kind. The conspirators' efforts to mobilise mass support were childish. They believed their barrage of resignations on May 14th would bring the people onto the streets: in fact, the people ignored them with lofty contempt. They planned to send agents to create disturbances in the mosques, but no such agents materialised. They expected to suborn

Radio Cairo to play stirring music to get the masses in the right mood, but they had no means of doing so or of ensuring the improbable effect they desired. The really impressive and dangerous achievement of the conspirators was their creation and manipulation of a secret apparatus within the ruling institution, the Arab Socialist Union. But this was a small group, as we have seen, of less than a hundred officials, who were incapable of implementing a coup and could only have worked slowly, like a cancerous growth, to wreck the body politic. The Corrective Revolution denied them the time they needed.

Sadat's show-down with the conspirators inaugurated constitutional reform. It is too early in the making of the historical record to decide whether Sadat was right to ascribe it to his own long-term conception of the course of the Egyptian Revolution. Perhaps this was a *post factum* rationalisation. Perhaps the clash began as a personal or factional power-struggle which then took on constitutional significance. But at the very least it crystallised Sadat's constitutional thinking and launched him on a reformist course.

The Corrective Revolution was in the first instance a purge of personnel. But it was measures, not men, that mattered most. The days of May established Sadat's position at the helm of the state; they dismantled or helped to dismantle some of the most menacing 'power centres'; and they made it possible, as the president said, for the people to recover mastery of their country — that is, for democratic institutions to be forged to replace the 'sultanate' and 'pashadoms' of preceding years. The constitution of 1971 was the symbol of this, enshrining the supremacy of law, the inviolability of personal liberty, the prohibition of arbitrary imprisonment, the proscription of torture. The mere existence of a permanent constitution was a great victory for democracy and liberty. Sadat's anniversary speech that year on the commemoration of the July Revolution expressed the new mood with its assurances that red tape would be eliminated and internal espionage and manhunting ended. The burning of taped telephone conversations, to which we have already referred, cauterised a national wound. The anniversary of the Corrective Revolution has become an Egyptian national holiday.

Sadat could not have piloted his Corrective Revolution through the A.S.U. (controlled, as it was, by his enemies), the army and the

National Assembly without great skill. Nor could he have managed it without the appeal to Nasser's memory and a plausible claim to be carrying on 'along the path of Nasser' [*Al-Akhbar*, 4th October 1970]. The blueprint for a more open society and a mixed economy had been adumbrated in Nasser's later years [Cooper 1982, 44]: in that sense, Sadat was genuinely closer to Nasser than self-professed Nasserists like Ali Sabry, who continued to adhere to the policies of an earlier and economically unsuccessful phase of Free Officer rule. Nor could Sadat have succeeded without popular support and allies among the élite: he found the former among the classes who had demanded liberalisation under Nasser, the latter among the growing legions of technocrats and, at the highest levels, among the liberals and progressives who had served, under Nasser, in Zakariya Muhiaddin's government and were excluded from power and patronage by Ali Sabry's domination of the A.S.U. Within four months of the Corrective Revolution, Sadat was able to follow up with sweeping changes in the law and personnel: 60 new laws by decree within eight weeks from mid-September; 1,237 new appointments in September, October and November [Cooper, 1982, 75-77]. This 'complete re-structuring', as Cooper has called it, shows not only the thoroughness of Sadat's achievement, but also how that achievement was built on Egypt's preparedness for change. Sadat had acted as a catalyst. With enthusiasm and drive, he had speeded and completed a process which his predecessor had begun with resignation and reluctance. He had exploited and rewarded a ready-made body of support.

This was not, of course, the end of Sadat's battle for democracy; it was scarcely the beginning of the end. It was, perhaps, the end of the beginning. It remained to create a party system and a critical yet constructive opposition; and the democratic state had to be built gradually. The anarchy of factional strife or the opportunism of anti-democratic groups could all too easily cut short an excessively precocious growth.

For eight years after 1971 Sadat sought the narrow overlap between liberty and order. In June 1971 he began a democratic reorganisation of the single ruling party, the Arab Socialist Union — a reorganisation the Sabry plotters had hoped to forestall. He wound up the secret apparatus and intelligence cells in which the May conspiracy had germinated. He took appointments to the Central Committee into his own hands. In the general election for the National Assembly in November 1971 there were no official A.S.U. candidates and nearly a third of the elected representatives came from outside the party, while more than half held no post in the party hierarchy. Sadat's efforts to open up politics evidently had popular support. In January 1971 political rights were restored to 12,000 disfranchised victims of political or class discrimination. These were just the opening moves in Sadat's campaign to remobilise Egyptian politics on a democratic footing.

Sadat was particularly anxious that Egyptian democracy should tolerate rival groups contending for power (although at first he eschewed the word 'parties' with its pre-revolutionary echoes), because, as he has said, single-party experiments under Nasser all tended towards totalitarianism [Sadat, 1978, 131]. But the cup of liberty was not like coffee powder, to be instantly infused. The aftermath of the Corrective Revolution, the preparations and consequences of the war of 1973, the delicate early stages of the road to peace — all these were trials for Egypt that exacted the maximum in national unity. Only gradually could the potentially disruptive effects of multi-party experiments be faced. The first stage of the process was the encouragement of dialogue within the single party, the Arab Socialist Union, which had been inherited from the previous régime. Sadat hoped to encourage each political tendency that manifested itself in dialogue to develop into an organisation.

At first these protean parties were to be formed from within the A.S.U. and to remain under its aegis. Sadat called them 'pulpits' or 'cathedrae' *(manabir, minbar)* — a characteristic choice of term, for it has a religious flavour, and there was certainly something evangelical about Sadat's zeal for democracy: western writers usually use the colourless translation, 'platforms'. The platforms were projected in 1975 by Sayid Marai, speaker of the People's Assembly, who was related to Sadat by marriage; the president was apprehensive lest they should afford an opportunity for Marxists or religious extremists to undermine his work, but decided tentatively to espouse the idea of platforms as a step towards democracy and a further blow to the 'power centres'. Formal inauguration of three platforms followed in January 1976 — with a centre group endorsing government policy and other groups to the right and left. Already by April Khalid

Muhiaddin's left-wing platform was formulating policies critical of the government and issuing statements attacking Sadat's abrogation of the Soviet friendship treaty.

Free competition of rival political views was thus current in the earliest days of Sadat's first democratic experiment. Opposition — like Athene though hardly, perhaps, so wise — was sprung fully armed. The October election of 1976 was fought by contending candidates from the three platforms in an atmosphere closer to multi-party democracy of the western sort than had been known in Egypt since the July Revolution. The achievement was warmly applauded in the western world and helped Sadat's political and economic westward *infitah.*

From a domestic Egyptian viewpoint, the elections appeared less satisfactory [Cooper, 1982, 204-34]. The platforms had been established and their principles defined by government committee; a host of self-defining platforms which had sprung up when the project was first mooted, and which had been announced in the press, were swept aside by *octroi.* The programmes of the platforms had been characterised officially as respectively of the left, right and centre. This was a foreign scheme of classification into which Egyptian politics fitted uneasily. Religious parties, in particular, belonged outside it and most candidates who espoused a distinctly Islamic political programme fought as independents. Forty-nine independents were actually elected, but Islamic factions still felt alienated and excluded. The elections were in no sense rigged, but the identification of the government with the centre and the unequal distribution of resources of finance, organisation, propaganda and influence helped to determine the outcome. The opposition was left frustrated and embittered with a smaller proportion of seats than of votes. In the circumstances, it was remarkable that the opposition's share of the vote in urban areas should have been as high as thirty-seven per cent. There was therefore evidence — if read aright — of considerable hostility to the government in areas which, within three months, would breed Egypt's worst riots since the revolution of '52. Sadat, however, failed to read the signs. He took the overwhelming statistical victory of the centre as mere confirmation of the huge plebiscite victories he had already won.

The food-price riots encouraged by communist agitators in

January 1977 therefore took him by surprise, but against the background depicted by Cooper, they now look intelligible. The Egyptian people are easily agitated: they are numerous, overcrowded, overwhelmingly young and riven by terrible extremes of wealth and poverty, education and illiteracy. Severe public disorders are endemic. Hardly a year goes by nowadays without at least some localised breakdown of public order. It is a measure of the success of Sadat's internal politics that economic and political discontents have largely ceased to generate riots. But it is a measure of his failure in a crucial field that religion has arisen in their place. The 'Islamic Renaissance' has inspired fanaticism, bigotry and hatred. The violence it has caused is the biggest single threat to Egypt's internal stability today. It is arguable that the riots of January 1977 were the last of the strictly economically inspired disorders and forerunners of the wars of religion waged annually in Egyptian city streets since then. Hopwood has expressed justifiable doubts that the riots represented a threat to Sadat's policies: it did seem that 'the people were asking for full stomachs rather than changes in policy' [Hopwood, 1982, 109]. And Mark Cooper witnessed variegated groups of rioters confusedly pursuing different targets and apparently expressing different discontents [Cooper, 1982, 242]. Sadat's reaction was to play down the importance of the riots, ascribe everything to communist agitators (who were certainly involved) and to put new vigour into the peace process: beyond peace, he was looking to an economic take-off to satisfy the urban masses. But the elections of 1976 had shown that substantial numbers of malcontents in the towns could be mobilised to oppose the government, and the January riots brought this home to Sadat. He therefore decided not to curtail progress towards democracy, but to proceed cautiously, without giving too much away to opposition parties and without allowing a handle to the violent and destructive opposition forces that had taken to the streets. The problem this decision left him was to identify those forces and set the right limit to democratic advance. Over the next few months the expectation that the platforms would become fully fledged parties was fulfilled. At the same time, the government embarked on the next stage by permitting new parties to join the three erstwhile platforms, even if the initiative for their creation should come from outside the A.S.U. The new law of 1977 laid down the following conditions for the formation of new parties:

- they must be approved by the Central Committee of the A.S.U.;
- they must have at least 20 deputies in the People's Assembly;
- half their founder members must be farmers or workers;
- they must not have existed under the monarchy;
- they must not be organised along regional, racial, or religious lines;
- they must subscribe to 'socialism, national unity and social peace' (this was a broad and elastic requirement designed only to exclude groups who were openly committed to violent change);
- their policies must differ from those of existing parties.

Only the second, fifth, and last of these conditions were restrictive — the others were purely formal or easy to comply with or elude; and the fifth and last were sensible and salutary measures, essential for national unity. The second condition, while it did impose a limitation in democracy in the sense of making a proliferation of parties unlikely, did not by any means preclude the formation of any new grouping, since the three existing parties were very broad churches indeed, from which secessions were likely, and there was a good number of independent deputies from whom a new party might recruit members.

In the event, it was of just such a combination of independents and secessionists that a new party was indeed formed. We must look carefully at this curious and illuminating episode. The New Wafd, which began to coalesce in May 1977, and achieved formal recognition in January 1978, was the first freely constituted party to gain official acceptance in Egypt since the July Revolution. It originated outside the A.S.U. and even largely outside the People's Assembly. It was in the ranks of the Egyptian Bar Association that it first became discernible to the public at large — an interesting milieu for such a development to occur in, since Sadat had always esteemed the legal profession and was proud of restoring lawyers' importance in Egyptian life by restoring the rule of law.

The occasion was a speech before the Association in August 1977 by Fuad Seraggedin, a caricature pasha of the *ancien régime* and leader of the pre-revolutionary Wafd, who with his tubbiness, his rich cigar, his (now discarded) fez and his wealth had seemed a compendium of symbols of an old, departed Egypt. But he was also a man of outstanding ability. His speech was an excoriating attack on the July Revolution and in particular the Nasser years; he could not conceal his grudging admiration for Sadat or his appreciation of the liberalisation that made his own outspokenness possible. But implicit in what he said was a desire to undo the revolution's work in everything except land reform [Reid, 1979, 390].

The New Wafd's programme when it emerged was less reactionary than this initial battle-cry. The membership of the party, pieced together from the ranks of existing deputies to achieve the minimum of 20 deputies demanded by law, was too diverse and too realistic to admit a policy so depressingly retrospective. The party found little rational ground on which to differ from presidential policy; but it did produce a programme which differed from the government's, in two respects, albeit only in degree. First, there was a difference of degree over the question of Egypt's relations with the Arab world. Sadat's government had already withdrawn from the immoderate pan-Arabism of the 'sixties and had emphasised Egyptian priorities; the president, as we have seen, made it his own mission to cultivate Egyptians' national self-awareness.

But the New Wafdists went further in attacking the very idea of Arab nationalism, relegating what they called the 'Arab peoples' (rather than 'people') to a vague linguistic and cultural grouping. Sadat's objection to this was of course, privately, on grounds of expediency rather than of principle. Secondly, they attacked the drive for industrialisation the government had led since the revolution, advocating instead the primacy of the agricultural sector. Again, Sadat had no fundamental objection to this: indeed, the Wafdists were anticipating a policy on which he was already resolved. It was through theft of his thunder that they posed their greatest threat.

Sadat reacted with caution to the formation of the New Wafd. In effect, the party contravened the stipulation of the 1977 law that no parties that existed under the monarchy should be revived. It was galling to have the achievements of the revolution threatened while they were still incomplete. In particular, the president hastened to rebut Fuad Seraggedin's abuse of the events of July 1952. Sadat pointed out that popular support was the essence of revolution and that it was by popular acclaim that the events of 1952 had been legitimised [Israeli, 1320].

The composition of the party was redolent of opportunism. Even some leftists had joined, ostensibly to help the party to the 'threshold' of 20 members in the People's Assembly, or to convert it from within; but they made uneasy bedfellows with the monarchists and old Wafdists and critics of the government from the right who formed the party's core. On the whole, the rapid eclipse of the New Wafd in 1978, when it was shown to have little electoral support, came as a relief. Briefly, what happened was that on March 28th, 1978, a neo-Wafdist deputy, Ashur Muhammad Nasr, lost his temper in the People's Assembly during a heated debate on food policies, when the Speaker waved down his attempt to make a speech. He created a commotion, shouting, "Down with President Sadat!" This unparliamentary interjection led to his eviction from the Assembly, and in the ensuing by-election the New Wafd was easily unseated by the government candidate. Sensing that the popularity of the government virtually nullified their electoral prospects, the New Wafdists decided to admit defeat and disband. Still, despite its early extinction, the episode of the New Wafd marked an important signpost along the democratic road. It had not helped to make the political system more representative or extend the people's voice in the legislature or the government, for it had too little support among the electorate. It did, however, contribute to the continuing multi-party experiment, to the vivacity of political debate, and to the extension of the range of expressed and canvassed political views.

Though Sadat was always suspicious of the neo-Wafdists' motives, he reacted to their criticisms in a responsive, constructive spirit. He accepted some of their specific demurs from government policy, cancelling, for instance, the inauspicious commercial development project for the Pyramids Plateau, returning a tax law to the People's Assembly for amendments to curb the activity of speculators. As for the question of the relationship of agrarian and industrial priorities, we shall see how the president had already anticipated his critics with an early reassessment. Even so, though Sadat's reaction to the Wafdist *revanche*, was intelligible and excusable, it presents puzzling aspects. It suggested that he was not entirely immune from infection by political expediency. It showed that he could fix the limits of liberty and democracy pretty narrowly when he felt threatened. It was a 'strong-man' reaction typical of a recurring theme in Sadat's statecraft, exemplified by the 'Corrective Revolution' at the start of his presidency and the unashamed purge of over 1,500 enemies in September 1981, near its end. Sadat was a genuine lover of democracy — he was its genie and its Ghazi, conjuring it into existence and protecting it in the hesitant, tentative years of its early growth. But, like all genies, he could act randomly at times; and, like all Ghazis, he tended to turn protection into a fairly tight form of tutelage. Sadat-style democracy had, it can fairly be alleged, a strong constructive tendency towards dictatorship, or at least the periodic exercise of dictatorial methods.

If there were excesses in the treatment of the New Wafd, for instance, it must be said on Sadat's behalf that he had a historic abhorrence of pashadom; he had already had one success against its revival in the form of power centres. He could not bear to see it arise anew in a guise recognisably that of pre-revolutionary years. He believed that he was fulfilling the revolution: he therefore maintained his enmity towards avowedly counter-revolutionary elements. And even in the 'purge' of 1981, when his main adversary was Muslim fanaticism, he took the opportunity to mop up pockets of Wafdist survival. Anti-Wafdism was a deep-seated prejudice of Sadat's — at least as deep as his commitment to democracy.

Two reservations made that commitment less than total. Sadat's insistence on his divine mission made him feel that he was in a sense empowered by divine election. The Egyptian political system, as interpreted by Sadat in innumerable speeches, enhanced this sense by setting the president on a lofty pedestal from which he could legislate by decree and on which he was virtue immune from criticism. The traditional Egyptian popular model of leadership enhanced it further: the *Rais* was popularly regarded as awesome and absolute, so that even a president like Sadat, who had come to the office without any charismatic pretensions, was rapidly invested with numinous and despotic qualities or, at least, given an opportunity to display them. Neither his temperament nor his circumstances permitted Sadat to renounce this role. He espoused democracy as an alternative to the arbitrary system of the 'sixties, not in preference to his own direct power; he saw himself as guiding it from above, raising it to maturity

Sadat, aged thirty, with his second bride, Jihan,
May, 1949.

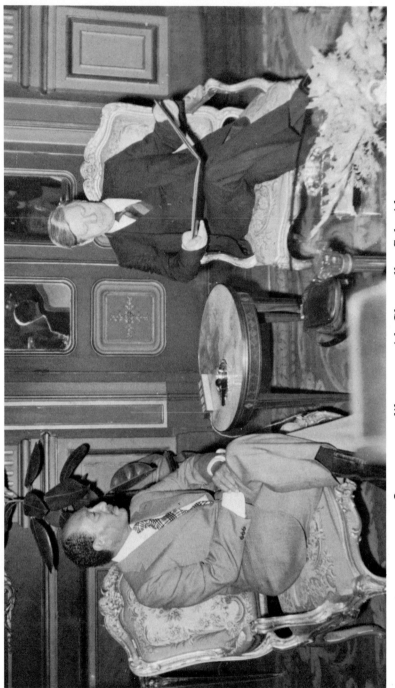

In statesmanlike pose with Chancellor Schmidt.

Sadat, the prayerful mystic, with the famous 'prayer-bump' showing on his forehead.

Sadat's favourite photograph of himself, in uniformed solemnity.

Opening the Ahmad Hamdi tunnel, named after another 'hero of the crossing' of October, 1973. Husni Mubarak is on Sadat's right.

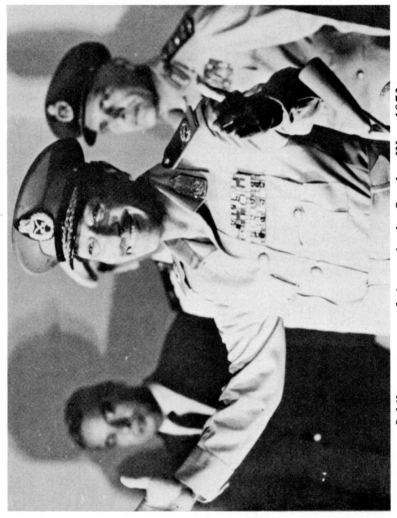

Jubilant at news of victory in the October War, 1973

Returning Israeli salutations in November, 1977.

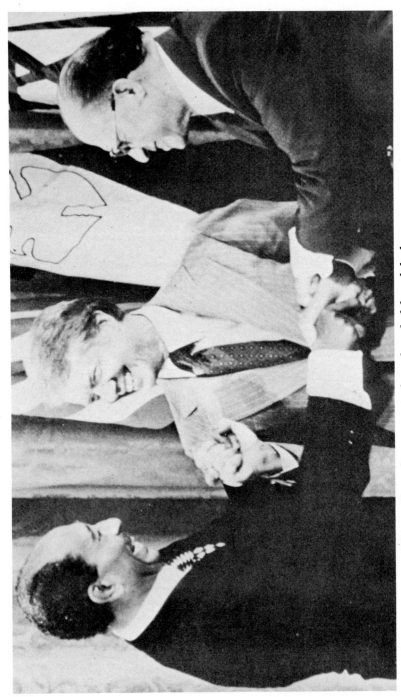

The smiles of success: a three-handed handshake means peace.

in paternal fashion. Furthermore, his enthusiasm for parties was always qualified. In the *October Paper* of 1974, in which he set out what he saw as the future course of the Egyptian 'Revolution', he roundly declared himself opposed not only to the single-party state but also to the 'fragmentation of national unity' by contending parties. He had not discarded this view by 1976, when he promised that the 'platforms' would be succeeded by parties. His declaration in the *October Paper*, though superficially illogical, was carefully prepared and frequently repeated. He never withdrew it; rather, he developed a conception of a political party which was peculiarly his own. Throughout the rest of his presidency, he insisted that opposition parties must conform to that conception. They must not be factious; they must make constructive criticisms; they must seek to influence the government rather than displace it; ideally, they should be led by his friends, even his relations. This may sound like a conception of party more appropriate to a Hanoverian monarch than a modern president, but in Egypt, which had no tradition of constructive opposition, it was not altogether inappropriate, especially during the transitional phase towards democracy, which, Sadat believed, Egypt was in. President Mubarak has tried to dispense with some of the checks on democracy that Sadat left intact or re-introduced towards the end of his life. Opposition newspapers have been revived; dialogue with opposition parties has begun anew. But the results have been depressing: energies diverted into sterile debate, with accusations of bad faith, electoral fraud and 'intellectual terrorism' *[Akhbar al-Yom*, 29th May 1982; *Al-Akhbar*, 30th May 1982; *Al-Ahali*, 14th July 1982].

The episode of the New Wafd showed how the government's willingness to imbibe the lessons of constructive criticism, while controlling the outlets through which it was expressed, has perhaps been an even more important element in the development of Egyptian democracy than the diversification of the party system. And possibly more significant still has been the emergence of a western-style opposition. We have already seen how the left-wing tendency within the A.S.U. constituted a vocal and tolerated, if not particularly helpful, opposition as early as April 1976, and how the interlude of the New Wafd contributed in 1977-78. But even before the first multi-party experiments, the People's Assembly was a lively forum: there was always a parliamentary opposition, throughout Sadat's presidency; at times, the legislature has acted to curb or criticise the executive. In December 1972, for instance, the Assembly expressed dissatisfaction with government policy and disbelief in the prime minister's assurances that plans for war with Israel were complete; the poor state of Egypt's relations with Russia was also attacked [*Arab Report*, 15th December 1972].

At the same time the Assembly, encouraged by Sadat, began to develop an important investigative role as a watchdog of democratic advance and citizens' rights, especially, for example, with its enquiries into sequestration abuses in which nationalisation or state custodianship of private property had caused hardship or cloaked corruption. Even a critic as exacting and as sceptical as Baker acknowledges the democratic vitality of the Assembly in this connection [Baker, 1978, 162]. After the demise of the New Wafd, the Socialist Labour Party of Mahmud Shukri began to show that it was no mere lapdog opposition. In September 1978 it intensified its anti-government line, calling for the abolition of remaining restrictions on parties and the press, the limitation of a presidential term of office to a maximum of five years, with more balanced relations with the super-powers and an effort to rebuild the mouldering edifice of Arab unity.

Of course a true democratic opposition, though it may begin in parliament, must not end there. The Socialist Labour Party has something approaching a mass organisation. Every popular political tendency in Egypt is allowed a voice in the press. And Sadat himself was a vector through which popular influence on the government was transmitted. From November 1971 he had meetings almost every week with representatives of grass-roots organisations, work forces, commerce, industry and farming. His frequent public appearances and the very style of his speeches, in which he appeared to think out loud before his people and lay tentative views before them for their consideration, was an invitation to feedback. He regarded his frequent speeches, discussion and question-and-answer sessions, especially with the Central Committee of the A.S.U. and with the People's Council, as part of democracy, a dialogue in which he would 'present, listen, and discuss' [Israeli, 322].

Every democratic system has its limitations: in a land where every individual were his own self-ruler without the restraining, guiding and equalising hand of the state to help him, life would indeed be

poor, nasty, brutish and short. It is important to understand where
the frontiers of Egyptian democracy stand today. In the first place, of
course, though the balance of the system is now clearly democratic, it
is still evolving. Democracy has in a sense been achieved; but that is
not to say that it will not be enhanced in future. Secondly, the
presidency itself retains a special dignity, partly because of the nature
of a democratic executive president. The constitution empowers him,
in exceptional circumstances, to act if he believes it necessary. Here the
Egyptian system resembles that of France. Any emergency measures
must be satisfied by plebiscite or the People's Assembly on the very
margins of democratic constraints.

Egyptian democracy has got beyond infancy but is still in
adolescence: Sadat was its tutelary genius, at its service but not at its
command. Moreover, the whole orientation of Egyptian culture, the
way of Egyptian life and thought, is paternalistic and familial. Sadat's
speeches expressed his relationship to the nation in the language of
that cultural world. He saw himself and was seen by his people as a
paterfamilias, endued with fatherly love and invested with fatherly
authority. The office of president has not yet been exposed to a
contested election of the sort which is now habitual for the People's
Assembly. Sadat was candid about his belief that the interests of
national unity at the time of the last presidential election in 1976
precluded a potentially divisive experiment. It is tempting to draw a
parallel between Egyptian and Chinese political evolution in the
twentieth century. Though Egypt's democracy aspires to conform to
western standards whereas China does not, there is scope for
comparison between Sadat's democratic headship in Egypt and Mao's
chairmanship — while he lived — in China, for both rose to power
through the ruins of a collapsed liberal-bourgeois revolutionary experiment; both ruled lands that were traditionally peasant monarchies;
both were peasants, buoyed up by popular, peasant support; both
were popularly invested with extraordinary, paternalistic power. The
most striking difference in the present connection is that Sadat used
that power to achieve democracy for his country; while Mao, the
more ideological of the two, became obsessed with arcane experiments
in sectionally based dictatorship that divided the nation and retarded
political and economic progress.

Another suggestive parallel is with Giscard d'Estaing: Sadat had none of the French president's aristocratic antecedents; the state he ruled had little of France's technological strength. But both countries have that important, large peasant element. And like Giscard, Sadat was a powerful executive president within a democratic framework. Giscard's example seems to have impressed Sadat himself. The Egyptian president copied the quasi-regal posture of his French counterpart, investing the headship of state with a numinous aura. In his last years he seemed almost to be trying to turn himself into an icon, abstracted from routine scenes, immured in the Abdin palace or the presidential rest-houses, swathed in mysterious *gallabiya,* immaculate suit or brilliant uniform, beautifully portrayed by some of the world's best photographers, *simplex munditiis.* This image was no mere affectation. Sadat felt he needed a certain dignity, a certain aloofness from the divisions — political and confessional — that increasingly bedevilled Egyptian life and marred Egyptian unity. It was something his wife wanted, too. She erred admirably in demigodising her husband and relishing aloofness. Arguably the adoption of a 'Giscardian' style was counter-productive. By compromising the popular character of the presidency it weakened Sadat's lines of direct contact with the people, who are often said, with some justice, to have felt bound to him by none of the impassioned solidarity inspired by other charismatic leaders.

The third area of qualification within Egypt's democratic system concerns the prohibition of political activity by communists, monarchists, atheists and religious fanatics. These are limitations on democracy, but they are justifiable — indeed, vital — if democracy is to be given a chance to thrive and prosper at all. In a world of hostile predators, only what Sadat called 'democracy with teeth and fangs' can survive. The experience of Germany in the 'thirties is enough to show that, in developing democracies anti-democratic forces should not be allowed democratic rights and privileges, for they will exploit them to conquer and destroy democracy. For Sadat, the major source of this sort of menace in his day was communism, which he utterly abhorred. He regarded it as incompatible with religion [Sadat, 1978, 284] and equated it with fascism because of its corporatist political philosophy and insensitivity to individual liberty: in both these totalitarian systems 'man's value is always determined by social needs' [Sadat, 1978, 83]. He said:

The communist policy goes against our three fundamental principles: national unity; the socialist solution, which includes democracy for the welfare of mankind; and social peace, because they have accepted bloody struggle and claim that it is class struggle which motivates history [*Arab Report,* 30th June, 1977].

It is curious how Sadat's historical sense, which we have had frequent call to notice, was offended by Marxism. His own study of history convinced him of the importance of individual activity and initiative in shaping events against the vast, impersonal forces to which historical determinism and dialectical materialism attribute all progress, indeed all change. One could say that his own epoch-making presidency served to verify his view. But the main thrust of his argument against communism was political rather than historical. He saw it as inimical to democracy and therefore to be curbed in democracy's interest. His reference to communism's incompatibility with national unity rests in his belief that it is an alien ideology that threatens the hard-won revival of Egypt's national spirit. That is why he called for 'an Egyptian left wing, not a Soviet one' and condemned Khalid Muhiaddin's United Progressive Party for 'buying foreign ideologies'.

Though it is hard to separate cause and effect, the limitation of communist activity in public life has been accompanied by communist subversion in recent years. For instance, nineteen communist plotters were prosecuted at the end of 1975; a further twenty were arrested in April 1976; communist agitators stimulated the riots of January 1977, against the government's decision to curtail food subsidies, and punitive action was taken against numerous communists and fellow travellers, especially within the student body, in the aftermath; in April 1978 nearly two hundred communists were tried for plotting the overthrow of the government; in October of that year about forty arrests were reported in connection with yet another communist conspiracy; and there were about fifty-six more such arrests in August 1979. Against this background, Sadat's unwillingness to suffer communists appears perfectly intelligible.

The government's unwillingness to allow religious parties must be understood against the backdrop of Egypt's history and the non-secretarian, *politique* nature of the Egyptian community. The history of the Muslim Brotherhood, which Sadat knew so well from his work with Hassan Banna in the 'forties, constitutes a cautionary tale against allowing religious groups to participate as parties in politics. Originally a devotional movement, aiming to inspire individual spiritual regeneration in the Brethren, the Brotherhood acquired political aims. In the 'fifties it threatened to replace Free Officer rule with a theocracy of mullahs of the sort that has more recently brought chaos to Iran: the brothers sought to substitute a crude Islamic fundamentalism for revolutionary and constitutional principles. Nasser proscribed the organisation. Sadat for most of the time allowed it to flourish as a genuinely spiritual movement and to exert political pressure through lobbying, petitioning and the press, but not to function as a party.

The Iranian experience confirmed him in this course. A theocratic form of government would in its way be as incompatible with democracy as communist rule. It would be particularly odious in Egypt, which, though the vast majority of its people share deeply felt Islamic convictions, has a large Christian minority who have always played a full part in national life and practised full toleration with their Muslim compatriots. As with the communists, religious fanatics have conspired against Egyptian democracy: there have been the terrorist acts and political murders of Takfir wal-higra, a secret society of sanguinary fanaticism unparalleled in Islam since the Assassins of the Middle Ages, and the plotted but aborted coup attempts of the equally fanatical and bloodthirsty organisation, Al-Jihad. Remnants of these groups, especially the latter, had a hand in the killing of Sadat.

The law of June 1st, 1978, has redefined the frontiers of Egyptian democracy. But it is important to understand that these are defensive frontiers, drawn to protect democracy against destruction from outside. Advocacy of doctrines opposed to what Sadat called 'the values of the country' — the principles, as the law says, of July 1952 and May 1971 — is banned. Effectively, in other words, monarchism, communism, atheism and fanatical sectarianism are excluded from government and the media. The liberties and privileges of democracy are limited to parties committed to the preservation and development of democracy. In this limited form, Egyptian democracy constantly recalled Sadat to the temptations of authoritarianism. One day, we may hope, thanks to timely vigilance exercised now, Egyptian democracy will become strong enough to tolerate anti-democratic forces and withstand them.

The law of 1978 was accompanied by an extension of press freedom and the abolition of the ministry of information. The press was already outspoken. Thereafter, until the emergency of 1981, it was not only free but also seen to be free. Meanwhile, the multi-party system became entrenched in the peculiar form Sadat devised, thanks to his initiative in disbanding and reconstituting the government party, under the name New Democratic Party, outside the umbrella of the A.S.U. organisation. The general election of 1979 was fought on a multi-party basis recognisably akin to the West German system and scarcely less democratic, by any standards, than anything to be found in the developing world. It was a 'foreign' package, imposed and controlled by the *Rais,* yet it helped to coax ahead the continuing process of bringing democracy to Egypt.

The Struggle for Prosperity

Of all the problems Sadat inherited from Nasser, the state of ruin to which Egypt's economy had sunk was the most daunting. Despite Egyptians' proud contempt of economic priorities, the fact was inescapable that every other form of progress depended on economic recovery. Economic needs overshadowed Sadat's presidency: he strove first to maintain the solvency of the government and the standard of life of the people; and then, as this battle was gradually, falteringly won, to build up resources, enrich the nation, and bring to ordinary Egyptians the prosperity which their efforts have merited but which they have never before attained.

The central theme of Egypt's modern economic history has been the tortuous transformation of a limited export economy based on primary products (and for a long time dependent on a single crop) to an industrial, diversified economy. Monarchy and revolution tried to expedite and force on this process in the absence of sufficient conditions, causing dislocation and disruption and neglecting the vital agricultural base. The problems of under-exploitation of the soil outside the Nile Valley, head-long population growth far exceeding disposable resources, in-built trade and payments deficits, and frequent bouts of war have all combined to make the general, long-term factors in Egypt's economic predicament over the last fifty years or so appear irredeemably bad. In addition, when Sadat came to power, a series of problems of more recent origin exacerbated the long-term difficulties. Above all, there was the tightening strain of war on Egypt's already excessively taut resources — not only the cataclysm of 1967, but also the slow, relentless bleeding of the Yemen war, an expensive piece of romantic pan-Arab adventurism by Nasser.

The import substitution programme, from which great results had been expected, was a failure. American aid had been withdrawn. Egypt had been forced to buy wheat on the international market. Military expenditure was absorbing nearly a third of national income. The Suez Canal was closed, its revenues lost. The National Debt was of alarming proportions — over $8,000 million were owed abroad, including perhaps nearly $4,000 million to Russia for war material. Diversification had made some progress: by 1968, for instance, Egypt was eighth in an export diversification table of fifteen selected developing countries, compiled by UNESCO, and had overtaken Argentina; but most diversification was within the 'agricultural basket' or in oil products. Re-allocation of labour away from agriculture had not benefited the industrial sector but had favoured relatively unproductive activities like services and the bureaucracy; public employees (fewer than 400,000 of them when Nasser came to power) numbered over a million by 1967; much of the skilled labour from Egypt's sophisticated educational institutions was being attracted away by more lucrative opportunities abroad. Economic planning — crucially important in view of Egypt's large public sector — had broken down as a result of the 1967 war.

The Aswan High Dam had not yet brought its expected benefits: its success depended on development of new industries to absorb its electricity — development which was delayed, industries which are only now achieving the required levels of capacity; the energy output of the dam is even today only three-quarters of what was projected at the time of construction and is sufficient to provide all Egypt's long-term energy needs. The dam had provided irrigation resources, but they could not be efficiently deployed to increase the amount of land under cultivation; it may even have contributed to the loss of yield caused by the rising water table. The problems of land reclamation were exacerbated by the encroachments of the western desert on the Nile valley and by the loss of fertile land to housing and urbanisation.

Food production had fallen per capita in the 'fifties and 'sixties —
production of sugar and grains was actually stagnant in absolute terms
in the 'fifties — and Egypt had been forced into dependence on foreign
wheat supplies to keep the people alive. Agricultural credit had
slumped because of the demands of war. Government liquidity was at
rock bottom, the wages of state employees threatened by the lack of
cash. The only encouraging features were the steady rise in oil
production, though even this had been dislocated by the loss of the
Sinai fields, and the abundance of young manpower in the country,
where half the population were under twenty-one years of age.

Although as a student of history Sadat rejected economic
determinism, against this distressing background it was imperative to
give early attention to increasing wealth and promoting growth. But,
as in Auden's *Spain,* it was a case of 'today, the struggle'. The
economy could be tinkered with; it could in some measure be
improved; but until the battle for liberation had been waged in Sinai,
the needs of the economy had to serve those of the coming war. In
fact, the war of 1973, though not waged for economic reasons,
brought redeeming graces to the economy. On September 30th, 1973,
Sadat told the National Security Council:

> Our economy has fallen below zero. We have commitments
> (to the banks, and so on) which we should but cannot meet
> by the end of the year. In three months' time...we shan't
> have enough bread in the pantry. I cannot ask the Arabs for a
> single dollar more [Sadat, 1978, 245].

Going to war in these circumstances represented a calculated risk.
Within a few weeks, Egypt had received hundreds of millions of
dollars in Arab and Iranian aid and the state's liquidity had been saved.
Over a longer term, the war made possible a political and economic
reorientation that brought access to more important sources of aid and
investment from the west.

After October, Sadat could turn in earnest to implementing
economic policies that offered real prospects of prosperity for Egypt.
This would be the 'era of the economic solution', with the
restructuring of socialist economic mechanisms to allow greater
freedom to individual efforts at creating wealth, combined with
infitah, an opening to increased economic relations with the west and
especially to western investment. This was the only policy consistent

with Egypt's long-term needs; shortages of capital, energy and food dominated the country's economic problems and would continue to do so — at the most optimistic projection — for more than a generation.

Only the western world could provide enough of these things: capital in the form of aid and investment; energy in the form of electronic and nuclear technology; food in the form of wheat. Sadat had been resolved on *infitah* ever since coming to power. Economic liberalisation had been foreshadowed in Nasser's last years. Only now could the policy assume priority and begin to produce results. Unashamedly, the objectives of the government were inseparably peace and prosperity — the people's reward after generations of toil and bloodshed, or, as the president's New Democratic Party put it in a slogan of 1978, 'food for every mouth, a house for every family, and prosperity for all'. Over a very long term, Sadat hoped to generate enough new wealth to sustain the sort of comprehensive social welfare programme the revolutionaries had dreamed of in 1952. But he knew that it would be a long, hard climb over the rainbow. Consumption would have to be controlled in order to allow investment and productivity to build up. Social welfare would have to be phased in at a rate the country could afford. After years of impoverishment, *infitah* would take time to work. Sadat did not conceal these realities from the people. In his May Day speech of 1974 he said:

> You, the workers, know better than anyone else that development, i.e. investment in manufacturing ventures, is the only solution to the problems of the masses, because they increase production and job opportunities...All nations that have suffered the way we did have resorted to the same measures; they were wise enough not to spend their resources on consumption right away...Rather, they elected to maintain a balance between their needs and constructive activity in order to ensure continued prosperity...It would be dishonest to allow a growth of income that exceeds the worth of production and services...In other words, I want you to face reality and increase productivity before we ask for the increase of our income [Israeli, 532-33].

The parallels which Sadat had in mind and at which he hinted in these words were those of post-war Germany and Japan: the consum-mation he desired for Egypt was an 'economic miracle' led by foreign investment; there were even fleeting but rapidly disappointed hopes of an Arab equivalent of Marshall aid for Egypt. His reading of history convinced him that it was not just foreign capital but gruelling endeavour and a productivity-centred ethos and effort that brought about Germany's and Japan's success. As in March 1976, citing the German example, he warned the Egyptian people that they needed 'five more hard years of sweat and toil to improve our economy' [*Arab Report*, 31st March 1976].

Three themes stand out as original and significant in Sadat's policy initiatives towards the achievement of prosperity in the post-October period. The first is economic liberalisation, comprising encouragement to the private sector at home and opening up investment opportunities for foreigners. Sadat remained loyal to the 'socialist solution' espoused by the Free Officers in the 'fifties. He insisted that the public sector must be preserved, must continue to constitute the greater moiety in the national economy, and must continue to enjoy investment priorities. But his was a moderate, mixed-economy socialism on the western European model. He shunned doctrinaire policies that put the redistribution of wealth ahead of its creation. He allowed fiscal incentives to be offered to capitalists and even permitted some private investment in the public sector. Above all, consistently with his political as well as his economic liberalism, he redressed all the accumulated grievances of the years of precipitate nationalisation and 'state guardianship' in the 'sixties, making it possible for the courts to compensate victims and in cases of abuse restore sequestrated property to its rightful owners.

In the field of foreign investment, *infitah* was symbolised by Law 43 of 1974, which provided broad tax exemptions for new companies and exemptions from profit-sharing laws for foreign firms. This took a long time to register success. The region's unstable reputation, the slow maturation of the peace process of 1973-79, the tedium of officious and bureaucratic delays in an Egyptian administration that Sadat had been gradually streamlining, the patchiness of the Egyptian labour markets and the unreliability of some areas of communications (especially telephone and public transport) in Cairo in the 'seventies, all tended to deter investors and make parturition long and painful. For most of the first two years of *infitah*, western private investors were reluctant to do more than sell management expertise and equipment. Tourism and construction projects, however, soon began to attract finance, and above all, especially in the context of the Lebanese civil war and the collapse of Beirut as an international financial centre, banking and finance moved to Egypt in a great migration of capital in the second half of the 'seventies. With time, this phenomenon may come to appear as significant as the drift of capital from Mediterranean to northern Europe in the early modern era. At the moment, with so much of the world economy wavering between inflation and recession, it is too early to judge the success of the *infitah*. But it is not too early to approve its wisdom. It has been the only possible realistic course in an Egyptian economy for which there could be no *fará de se*.

The second theme has been the administrative decentralistion of development. Legislation to accomplish this was launched in 1975. Sadat's conception of economic administration was its basis: the president believed firmly in central planning, but saw the apparatus of the state as the servant of the people, not their master; the ideas for development should therefore emanate from the localities, be centrally co-ordinated, and returned to local authorities for execution. Seventy-five per cent of taxes were earmarked for local development projects. The third theme of Sadat's policy was connected with this economic devolution. His reassessment of Egypt's industrial and agrarian priorities in 1976 was partly a response to local expressions of views.

Of course, other factors intersected: Egypt's appallingly low crop yield; the adverse effects on national sovereignty of dependence on imported food; the growing global importance of food products; the growth of the rice crop in Egypt, offering a prospect of escape from the cycle of deficiency in nutritional cereals; the lack of demand abroad for Egyptian manufactures; the chances of marrying Egypt's industrial and agrarian sectors by concentrating on agricultural machinery and other agriculture-related industries; the hope that yields could be improved by increased mechanisation. So, on July 22nd, 1976, Sadat announced:

> I have taken a strategic decision...designed to switch most of
> our development to agro-industrial complexes, for we had
> neglected the development of modern, mechanised
> agriculture...In a few years, foodstuffs will be more

important than oil or industrial goods [Israeli, 1325].

To switch away from industrialisation would be folly. Egypt's economic situation is in many ways the most propitious in the third world for the accomplishment of a new industrial revolution: her geographical position (which makes her an ideal *entrepôt*), her manpower resources, her educational institutions, and the presence of the High Dam mark her for such a role. On the other hand, the unrestrained enthusiasm for industrialisation which ignited Egypt's economic planners after the July Revolution caused agriculture to be undervalued and the slow but relentless retraction of Egypt's agrarian base to be overlooked for too long. Sadat seems to have struck the right balance.

It is easy to deride *infitah* by pointing to the worst of its side-effects — the growth of a new-rich class of entrepreneurial middlemen and a *demi-monde* of wealth allied with graft that impedes efficiency and alienates ordinary people. But this is not the result directly of the policy, rather of unforeseeable defects in its execution. It is less easy for critics to say what else Sadat should have done. Economic liberalisation and a bid for foreign aid could not accomplish all that Egyptians asked of them. But they could and did achieve more for the prosperity of the people than any other policy. They were imperfect, like every modern economic nostrum. They could not be applied except through trial and error — sometimes a great deal of error. But they were the only realistic options. In embracing them with characteristic enthusiasm, Sadat was making a virtue of necessity.

Improvement in the resources situation and in the performance of the economy has followed a course closely in step with the peace process. The reopening of the Suez Canal in 1975 was symbolic of a return to 'business as usual'. With the return to normalcy and the prospect of peace, commercial confidence was rekindled and the cycle of wealth creation started up again.

The economy was like some great hibernating beast, slowly and tentatively stretching its limbs and flexing its muscles after a long spell of sleep. Between 1975 and 1977, Canal traffic almost doubled; over the same period, G.N.I. rose by more than 15%. The balance of payments deficit fell by more than 17%. New resources — especially of oil — transformed Egypt's industrial and energy prospects: in 1976, for instance, oil finds were registered in the Red Sea and the Gulf of

Suez; the peace process began to lead to the recovery of the Sinai oilfields. Three new offshore fields were opened in 1977. A veritable bonanza was found in the eastern desert in March 1978, and more offshore production was inaugurated in April. Since then, Egypt has become the world's fastest-growing source of oil and the site of some of the most productive new fields. Egyptian oil policy, sniping from outside OPEC at the doctrine of stinted output, has been able to exploit high prices while maximising returns.

That April, Sadat went on an 'economic tour' — a presidential visitation of a representative range of important projects that were building up the country's wealth base for the future. A review of his itinerary admirably illustrates the concrete realities of his economic policy. At Dishna, Sadat saw a new sugar refinery; at Nag Hammadi, a new aluminium industry complex, which confirmed him in the view that 'the prospect of industry in Egypt is promising'. At Suhag he saw a new university hospital; at Hurghada, an ice plant, two new trawlers and twenty-five fishing-boats; at Safaga, a new port; in the Red Sea region generally, 1,500 feddans of reclaimed desert land and plans for the development of tourism; at Abu Simbel, he visited the Toshka Canal; at Aswan, a food-sufficiency project. And in the western desert generally he reviewed reclamation plans designed to add food production to mineral exploitation as a feature of the region's economic importance. The president hoped one day to see the desert become a settled region, with population redistributed from the overcrowded Nile valley; in this peripheral and traditionally neglected wasteland, he said, 'Egypt's future lies' [*Arab Report,* 15th and 30th April, 1978]. In fact, the future of this part of his legacy looks promising. Egypt is in the throes of one of the biggest planned demographic experiments in history, breaking the Egyptian people's traditional confinement within the Nile valley and settling areas of desert, some never before populated, some unpopulated since Pharaonic times.

Many indicators continued favourable in 1978 — especially the 9% growth rate and improved hard currency reserves. But much of the long-term nexus of problems remained as tight and complex as ever, and there were some new difficulties — in particular, an inflation rate of 30%, and pressure from the I.M.F. to reduce the social costs of Egypt's budget, a sacrifice the government was unwilling to make. Political uncertainties clouded the economy. Only a swift resolution of the peace process could dispel these dark obnubilations. Yet Arab aid had already shrivelled; further progress towards peace would certainly provoke more hostile sanctions from intransigent and 'rejectionist' countries: the 600,000 Egyptians working abroad in Arab countries remitted $2,300 m. home in 1978, and this vital area of foreign earnings might be jeopardised.

By calling the rejectionist bluff in 1979 and concluding peace with Israel, Sadat actually strengthened the economy and launched it on a new phase of growth. The total severance of Arab aid was of no consequence; the Arabs had anyway reverted to unproductive parsimony once the euphoria of October was past. Saudi Arabia claimed to have given Egypt $7,000 m. in aid since 1973, but in 1978 capital aid from Saudi Arabia and Kuwait together amounted to only $35m. Few new sanctions of any consequence were forthcoming. The dissolution of the Arab Organisation for Industrialisation in July came as a blow, but the funds were frozen and Egypt took over the programme in her own right: the first projects undertaken by the new Egyptian Organisation for Industrialisation illustrated the effects of economic and political orientation towards the west and the benefits of peace in a vivid way — they were for the production of Swingfire systems and Lynx helicopters with British help and Mirage aircraft in collaboration with France.

Indeed, the peace treaty opened floodgates to aid from the developed and developing worlds. Increased annual loans were promised from the World Bank and Japan. An aircraft-exchange deal was announced with China in June. Indian-Egyptian economic co-operation got under way. In July, an important watershed was crossed when the first joint Israeli-Egyptian economic venture was revealed — co-operation with Ko-or Industries of Israel in the fields of agricultural equipment, solar energy, oil refining and medical electronics. Among loans announced in August were $204 m. from the World Bank towards gas and electronics plant, $32.5 m. from the International Development Association for the tourist industry, $30m. from the U.S. Agency for International Development for cereals and $25 m. from the same source for Egypt's Agricultural Development Bank, $300 m. in economic aid from America and $3,700 m. in the U.S. arms-sales credits.

At the same time, America was helping to revitalise Egypt's

growing domestic arms industry, which was specialising in areas of productive economic spin-off, like electronic systems, rocket fuel, and optical systems. Evidently, American help was the key to progress, and the productive transformation of Egypt's relations with America must be laid to Sadat's personal credit. It was his own policy. His own perseverance and efforts materially helped in its elaboration. Once the right sort of relations were established, he was in the forefront of the campaign to secure aid, using his friendship with President Carter as a background for hard economic as well as political bargaining and appealing directly to the American people. On March 27th, 1979, he told businessmen in Washington of Egypt's three catchwords: peace, democracy and prosperity. 'With the help of President Carter we have achieved peace; democracy is my responsibility, but for prosperity I count on your help' [*Arab Report*, 11th April, 1979].

Modern economic problems are too vast for one man to resolve. No government, much less any single leader, has achieved mastery over the economic factors which impinge on a country's life. But Sadat's contribution to Egypt's recovery does seem to have been of exceptional weight. He tracked policies which exploit favourable conditions to the full with a virtually unerring eye and he carried them out purposefully even when, as in the case of economic *infitah*, the rewards were slow to follow. The quality of his statecraft which made this possible was surely his realism.

It was a hard decision to force through *infitah;* it was a hard decision to defer social objectives in the interests of building up a strong economic infrastructure, amply nourished with investment for the future. Yet these decisions were also the only ones that could confront the realities of the long-term demographic, financial and energy-related difficulties that overshadowed Egypt. The economic future is always inscrutable even to the expert augurs and astrologers who man the world's economic institutes. But at the very least Sadat earned a long reprieve and a prospect of prosperity for an economy that was in ruins when he took it in hand. His method was instinctive, like Roosevelt's. He chose the policies without ever understanding the economics that lay behind them.

* * *

The Search for a Better Society

Inequality and mass deprivation have been traditional features — indeed, have traditionally been the most conspicuous features — of Egyptian society. The July Revolution diminished these deficiencies but did not eliminate them. For instance, whereas in 1952 5.7% of landowners owned 64.6% of the land, in 1965 5.5% owned 42.9%. The great near-feudatories and territorial pashas of tradition had been relegated to the past, but a small minority of prosperous yeomen owning up to 50 feddans replaced them as a privileged class, dominating their poorer fellow peasants. Although 400,000 families benefited from the revolution's land reforms, for most their condition was ameliorated but not transformed. While some of the iniquitous old classes disappeared, others arose to replace them — a fortunate and sometimes exploitative bureaucratic élite, a relatively rich class of public sector managers, an industrial proletariat that had access to benefits available only in the towns.

Above all, among the social problems that faced Sadat when he assumed the presidency, was the fact that a society in which the benefits of prosperity were distributed in abundance to all was impossible in Egypt. National wealth was insufficient. Sadat had to achieve social justice on a shoe-string. There would not, in the economic circumstances, be enough for all; the task was to prevent any one class from getting a stranglehold on wealth and to prevent economic inequalities from overspilling into other areas and restricting equality of opportunity.

Sadat's basic social philosophy was genuinely socialist. He adhered firmly to the July revolutionaries' conception of the Egyptian nation as an 'alliance of active popular forces', that is, workers by hand and brain who live by their labour rather than unearned income. He remained loyal to principles he expressed clearly, for example, at a rally for May Day in Alexandria in 1972:

We live in a society where labour is the supreme value...We shall not restore class privileges and we shall never revert to the rule of capitalism. There will be no retreat from the sovereignty of the people over the means of production [Israeli, 197].

Of course, within such a broad alliance as that of the active popular forces there are bound to be great disparities. In recent years, all the vigilance the Egyptian government has been able to spare from the demands of wealth creation have gone on preventing and controlling exploitation. The self-enrichment of entrepreneurs and middlemen, socially divisive though it may be, has had to be tolerated in the broader interest of promoting national prosperity as a whole. Sadat accepted this with his habitual pragmatism. He put his faith in the still commanding position of the public sector, the good sense of the Eyptian people, and the universal awareness of the need for a period of adjustment before the benefits of growth can be fully enjoyed. He devoted many speeches to stimulating this collective sense of purpose and refrained from taking public measures to harry the rich gratuitously.

Though there have been public disorders — in January 1975, more seriously in January 1977, and periodically since then until the severe disturbances of 1981 — none attracted wide support. January 1977 saw the biggest wave of unrest, with severe riots in six towns, but that was provoked by withdrawal of food subsidies — an economy the government has avoided on a big scale ever since. Most of the time the people helped the president by showing the sort of patience and understanding he asked of them. Most of the discontented have remained resigned. Peasants and workers have reacted to the *embourgeoisement* of many of their fellow citizens indifferently, without rancour. The forbearance of the masses, especially the peasant masses from whom Sadat was sprung, has been a major factor in averting social upheaval.

Although the president tolerated and even encouraged, as a matter of necessity, the rise of an opportunistic, entrepreneurial class, he placed a firm curb on other sources of inequality and acted to expedite the circulation of wealth and the spread of social welfare. The bureaucracy, for instance, has long been a great unleveller in Egypt. The July Revolution took aboard so many new public responsibilities that the bureaucracy expanded almost uncontrollably, becoming bloated and glutted with power and manpower, commanding high salaries and positions of social influence and even dominance. Sadat treated this advanced case of bureaucratic hypertrophy by placing the public service on a strict regimen. Economy has been enforced. Efficiency has been improved. Training has been attuned to these tasks and a leaner, more dedicated and public-spirited bureaucracy has begun to take shape. Sadat entrusted Fuad Sharif with this programme and until his death in 1976 he responded superbly to the president's wishes, improving management not only in the administration but throughout the public sector, deploying the techniques and skills developed by modern business efficiency and public administration schools in America and Western Europe.

Public criticism of the bureaucracy has been used to curtail the complacency and arrogance to which an administrative élite can all too easily fall prey: in particular, Sadat accused the bureaucrats of impeding *infitah* — as is all too true, for the meshes of red tape could still deter enterprise and investment [*Der Spiegel,* 26th March 1976]. Corruption was a more serious problem than bureaucratic inertia. There is corruption in every system: all that differs is the degree to which it is denounced by the opposition or harried by the régime. Sadat, who had been acutely aware of the extent of corruption under Nasser, suffered from selective myopeia when beholding it under his own rule. He failed to exercise the necessary vigilance, so that corrupt and corpulent fortunes were made in his own party and even his own entourage. The trials of Rashad Uthman, local 'boss' and party stalwart who 'fronted' countless crimes, and of Sadat's own brother, Ismat, whose 'stench filled Egypt', have brought into the open the patchiness of Sadat's control. But Uthman, as a self-made man, was in part the victim of mandarin jealousy: his obscure provenance as a dock-hand and his lack of formal education attracted more criticism from some quarters in press and parliament than his avowed crimes. And Ismat was a token sacrifice. While Sadat lived, corruption was attacked with ardour both in the courts, whose efforts were directed against individual cases of abuse of public office for gain, and in the generalised criticism Sadat voiced in his speeches or which the government has encouraged in the press and other media. Naguib Mahfouz's prize-winning screenplay, for instance, *The Guilty Ones,* virulently savages corruption in a dramatically overdrawn but vivid and original whodunit, where the suspects, who as they are cleared of murder are revealed as guilty of other crimes or serious improprieties, are all bureaucrats or professional men.

The professions are in fact a social group whom Sadat sought to foster and integrate with the alliance of active forces. By restoring the rule of law he helped rehabilitate the lawyers — a class much reviled in the early years of Free Officer rule. The importance he attached to education has benefited teachers and researchers. Sadat was candidly aware that Egypt must respect and reward scientists, engineers, and doctors if the 'brain drain' from which the country has suffered for years is to be blocked and if social and economic objectives are to be realised. Similarly, if democracy is to thrive, writers must have a role. But perhaps no profession stood in more acute need of rehabilitation when Sadat came to power than that of soldiering. Sadat revolutionised the forces' morale and national status with the October War; he continued to nourish them with praise, a high level of investment in the armed services, and active deployment no longer in war but in civil projects of social utility.

Though the country was not yet able, by the end of Sadat's life, to afford a level of social spending which he would have viewed as adequate, the president deliberately took risks with relatively high budget allocations for social welfare, bringing the displeasure of the I.M.F. Today, rural health care and education are the priorities, for both had been emphasised heavily by the Free Officers, yet in neither area had much progress been made before Sadat became president. In health care, the problem is one of shortage of medical personnel. In the 'sixties the government tried to compel doctors to answer the needs of country people, but this approach was both illiberal and unproductive — a crime and a mistake, all at once. Sadat attempted a different approach, appealing to the doctors' social consciences, clamping down on bureaucratic harassment and wooing them with supplemental income and special training schemes. Rural health care still suffers because of the competition from more lucrative posts outside the country for the large numbers of doctors graduating from Egypt's numerous and excellent institutions of training, but at least the new policy has made inroads into the problem and there is now no locality that is entirely without medical services.

On the illiteracy front, Sadat inherited a really desperate situation: although Egypt enjoys better educational amenities than most of the emergent world, this is an area of public concern, where complacency is intolerable while imperfections remain. In the 'sixties, growth of population so far outstripped provision of increased school places that the numbers of eligible children not accommodated in school actually rose from 1.8m. in 1960 to the alarming figure of 2.06m. in 1970. In that year the illiterate proportion of the population was 60%. Since then, energetic remedial action by the government has helped the figures to improve. Illiteracy now afflicts only half the people and the battle to provide sufficient school places goes on. Ironically, high rates of illiteracy in Egypt have always favoured incumbent régimes — that of Sadat included. As sources of social differentiation, they are less easily exploited by opposition groups than cruder forms of class division or differences of religion or wealth. They make the rural poor less willing and less able to utter or respond to criticisms of the government than their more sophisticated brethren in the towns. Thus Sadat was able always to retain unqualified support in his rural constituency, even when there were riots or indifference in the towns. To his credit, Sadat did not try to prolong illiteracy, or foster it by neglect, as pre-revolutionary régimes had done.

There are some sources of social division which cannot be touched by efforts to diminish class differences and distribute social benefits equally. In Egypt, religion is an area of social concern. It has tended to complicate the social disadvantages suffered by women and has been a potential flashpoint between the Christian minority and the Muslim majority. Muslims and Copts have dwelt together in peace in Egypt for 1,300 years, but the pressures on both communities to rupture their long entente have increased in recent years. The Islamic renaissance has galvanised some Egyptians into a more militant and less tolerant Islamic awareness. Some instances of Christian evangelism have caused resentment. The law of the state — derived, as the constitution specifies, from Islam — has become more stridently Islamic, as the Christians have lost the loud voice in government they enjoyed before the Second World War: the only Christian deputies in the People's Assembly are now those nominated by the president. Christians have felt increasingly excluded and threatened, as Pope Shenouda's call for more Christian deputies has shown. And, in the background, the civil war in Lebanon has embittered Muslim feeling.

As a result of these pressures, the minority has suffered provocations. A keynote of terrorism in the campaign of the Muslim fanatics against the Copts was struck by the destruction of the oldest Coptic church in Cairo with an incendiary bomb in March 1979. Amid these perils, Sadat was a peacemaker at home, as on the international stage. He lost no opportunity to praise the Copts' sense of patriotism and brotherhood with other Egyptians. In 1977 he responded to a wave of minor provocations and demonstrations by joining the Coptic Pope at the inauguration of a new Christian hospital and declaring in October:

> All Egyptians — Muslims and Copts — have for generations taken part in our national battles for liberation and reconstruction...Plotters from outside our land do not know the nature of this people and the strength of their faith in God [*Arab Report*, 31st October 1977].

Sadat was motivated by more than his presidential duty and desire for national unity in coming to the Copts' defence. Their predicament appealed to him partly because of his personal sympathy with and knowledge of them, for he was educated in a Coptic school — a debt he felt deeply — and had long admired Coptic asceticism; partly, too, his belief in the common heritage of all the great monotheistic religions and his commitment to an inclusive 'love of all humanity' were engaged by the Copts' plight.

Though Egypt has had her share of mad mullahs, Egyptian Islam is fortunate to be served by a generally enlightened clergy and to possess a rational school of scriptural exegesis in Al-Azhar, whose shaikhs consistently supported Sadat in his efforts to make Islam an enlightening and modernising, rather than a cramping and retrograde, influence on the secular law. On the whole, superficialities do not pass for fundamentalism in Egypt as they do in some parts of the Islamic world. In recent years, Islamic reflections in new legislation have concerned areas of common sense, like public consumption of alcohol and the control of immoral displays. Egypt has been spared the barbarities of so-called 'traditional' punishments.

No area, of course, is more sensitive in connection with the social implications of the *Sharia* that the status of women, and here Sadat came under pressure from Islamic reactionaries who 'want to put women back into tents'. But the president was firm on this score: Islamic law must be liberally interpreted in favour of women; a form of inequality that relegates half the population — half the talent, half the energy, half the patriotism, half the will — to second-class status would be intolerable in modern Egypt. 'The state', he said, 'can only be reconstructed by sharing responsibilities between the sexes' [*Arab Report*, 15th April, 1979].

Women's equality has been the object of one of the most fervent and successful of the social campaigns of Egypt's former 'First Lady' (so called in imitation not directly of the American example, but of the Filipinio, where Mrs Marcos has been given an image and a role in the making of a developing nation). The president's wife helped Sadat — as we have seen — in a wide range of his activities, but it is her talent for social work that has marked out the terrain of her greatest contributions. No one supposes that she is immune from female vanities: naturally she loves to dress well, attract admiration, and indulge her own favourites among the many claims on her attention from charities and social projects. But her labours on the local councils of both her and her husband's native villages, her efforts on behalf of the war wounded, her contribution to the study and elaboration of rehabilitation programmes for the handicapped, her envolement in Children's Welfare projects, and her daily attention to scores of individual and social problems laid before her by correspondents who know that they could be sure of a compassionate hearing from her, all testify to the depth of her concern with her social image.

Her only big contribution to the statute book was the amendment she helped to draft to the Personal Status Law of July, 1979, on women's rights in divorce cases, dutifully approved by Shaikh Adl-Rahman Bizzar of Al-Azhar as compatible with the Sharia. Jihan's amendment protected women from secret arbitrary divorces which husbands had previously been able to take out without telling their wives and even without forgoing their continued services; it also enabled women's claims in the treatment of questions of property and custody of children in divorce cases to be considered on terms of equality with those of husbands. Her other major campaign for women called for more female deputies in the People's Assembly and led to seats being reserved for women in major cities; as a result, the 1979 general election brought thirty new women M.P.s.

The president's wife found what she thought was just the right role for a First Lady — helping to show women how to undertake wider social responsibilities without sacrificing their traditional values. It shows a typical moderation and pragmatism, worthy of the wife of

Anwar Sadat. In the same context, she showed tactical prowess equally worthy of her husband by calling on women M.P.s when the Personal Status Law was before the legislature and warning them — indeed, making them promise — to keep silent during the debate so as not to provoke controversy and invite crippling amendments.

The result of the complementary efforts of Sadat and his wife has been to make Egypt an outstanding example of the idea of equality among fellow citizens, especially in the context of women's rights. The law grants women thirty seats in parliament and ten to twenty per cent of seats on local councils. Nearly half the students in higher education are women: the number of working women increases by more than 16,000 yearly. The wives of Egypt have acquired for the first time a right to a divorce settlement and can opt out of polygamous marriages without losing everything — from their property to their children. The achievements of Sadat's policy on behalf of women nicely illustrate his belief in the necessity of seeking peace abroad in tandem with justice at home. Women's self-perceptions have genuinely changed. In modern Egyptian women's fiction they play active roles, still consistent with tradition [Suleiman, 1978, 369; see also Nahid al-Manchawi in *Al-Gumhuriya*, 10th October 1981].

There were, of course, problems Sadat was powerless to remedy and others which he tackled in the wrong way. He left behind him an Egypt still riddled with graft and inefficiency: personally incorruptible, he was naïve about the corruption of others, especially of those close to him whose loyalty he confused with honesty. He never faced up to graduate discontent and its consequences: in Egypt, the state guarantees employment to all who have tertiary education. The private sector mops up most of the best and pays them well. The state employs a sullen and resentful rump at subsistence wages. Sadat never projected the same image of 'caring', personal involvement with domestic policy as he did in foreign affairs: accusations of indifference were not entirely justified, but they were partly his own fault, since by delegating too much and indulging in visions of the future, sometimes apparently at the expense of present action, he glutted his critics. And, as everyone knows, he failed to deal decisively with the Muslim extremist opposition, whose enmity, though so far only mildly damaging to the state, would prove fatal to Sadat's own life.

CHAPTER FIVE

Years of Achievement Abroad

The Struggle for Independence

Sadat was only the second Egyptian to have ruled Egypt during the last two and a half millennia. In modern history, the one man to have shared a comparable experience in this respect was Gamal Abdel-Nasser. For the rest, Egypt has had Turkish, Mameluke, French, British and Albanian rulers in modern times, but to find another instance like Nasser's or Sadat's one must go back to the time of the Pharaohs. This extraordinary fact throws the period since the July Revolution into startling relief against the long era of foreign domination which preceded it and establishes a thread of continuity between pharaonic and contemporary Egypt, the strength of which we have seen already in numerous analogies. It is a fact which is bound to have affected Egypt, for no people can survive centuries of alien subjugation, uncowed, without struggles and sacrifices.

In particular, Sadat himself was personally affected by this feature of Egypt's history: the president's was an historical cast of mind, which concentrated on and conjured with the past, like an angler with his line. Sadat was profoundly aware of the elements of constancy — even, of serenity — that have underlain the apparently turbulent surface of the course of Egypt's history. He often spoke and wrote of these things: the people of Egypt, who, despite the conquests and colonisations that have threatened them or scarred them, are still the direct descendants of the same Egyptians who created and sustained an ancient civilisation; the spiritual and intellectual strengths which still far outstrip Egypt's material resources and which, Sadat believed, can be traced by uninterrupted descent to ancient times; the land of Egypt — the 'good land', as he always called it, when speaking of desert and Nile valley alike; the Nile itself, the central, vital artery, uniting different epochs of Egyptian history, combing in one polity the land it flows through and floods, ever since the unification of Upper and

Lower Egypt under the Pharaoh Den-Semti; and finally the 'sense of identity' which has helped to make Egypt what it is in every age and has preserved the same sense of mutual belonging by which Egyptians have distinguished themselves under every native dynasty and every foreign hegemony [Sadat, 1978, 204].

No aspect of Sadat's statecraft was as much influenced by this background of alien supremacy as his struggle to assert and make meaningful Egypt's independence; no achievement more deeply affected than his realisation or near-realisation of an ideal, cherished by the nineteenth-century nationalists and twentieth-century revolutionaries but never fully achieved, of an Egypt unconstrained by foreign power, able to formulate her own role and make her own way in the world. It is common to think of Egyptian foreign policy since the July Revolution as dominated by the problems of Palestine, but the quest for independence is an older and more fundamental objective — not just formal independence in the sense of exclusion of colonial powers and the exercise of self-government, but independence of action in the international sphere, where Egypt has potentially a great role to play: independence to formulate and pursue foreign policy without submitting to the tutelage or suffering the condescension of forces from outside the country. Sadat's own term for this genuine, thoroughgoing independence was 'the liberation of Egypt's national will' [Israeli 392].

For Egypt, the quest for independence has never been easy; super-powers have always felt the allure of her strategic position — Persia, Macedon, and Rome in ancient times, the Turks, French, and British in modern, and most recently the Soviet Union and the United States. Such powerful suitors can sometimes be parried; they can rarely be repelled; they can be wooed in the manner, say, of that other great Egyptian ruler, Cleopatra, but they can rarely be resisted. Even so intense a patriot as Nasser, who fought with breathtaking ardour to purge Egypt of forms of foreign control, could not elude thraldom to a super-power. Only Sadat succeeded or almost succeeded in totally freeing Egypt and Egyptian policy, prising the country from the super-powers' claws.

Sadat's commitment to the cause of Egyptian independence began in childhood in innocent hatred of British intruders who ran Egypt with their customary indifferent efficiency and benevolent arrogance.

Their paternalism was an insult to the young Sadat, the complacency with which they excluded Egyptians from their rights an outrage. He loathed, when he was at school in Cairo, as an authoritarian emblem, the fat, rubicund British policemen, their big knees bobbing up and down under their absurd shorts as, puffing, panting, and perspiring, they biked around the town, straining to adjust to an environment evidently not their own, in which they were both mountebanks and masters. Even before he had seen Britishers to hate, the young Anwar had imbibed from his mother and grandmother anti-British villagers' tales, in which fairy stories, epic myths, and true historical anecdotes combined in a rich, powerful, memorable form of oral literature. Many tales were of Zahran of Denshway — a largely apocryphal martyr, albeit one in whom Sadat's faith had always been sincere; but the dazzling mythopœia of the Egyptian people is irresistible in a good cause.

Through all the stories the British emerged as impersonal, demonic powers, wicked as goblins, strong as trolls, and strange and sinister as either, while of course more real, more substantial than both. And through the stories too came the intelligible goodness and solidity of Egypt and her people. 'Nothing', Anwar's grandmother told him, 'is as significant as your being a child of this land' [Sadat, 1978, 3, 5; Baker, 1978, 15]. As Sadat moved from his rural home to Cairo, as the childish chauvinist grew into an adolescent nationalist, the stories on which he had been brought up shed their husk of fantasy; they were illustrated, made real, enfleshed by thousands of daily enactments of life under British rule; for this foreign régime, though its harshness was mitigated by respect for the rule of law and its indifference to Egyptian dignity mollified by paternalism, was odious simply because it was foreign. An Egypt beholden to alien masters was intolerable to the generation among whom Sadat grew up. And his struggles and conspiracies against British rule in the early years of the Free Officers' Movement were the first stage of his contribution to Egypt's quest for independence.

Liberation from Britain was achieved by Nasser — was, indeed, in some ways, Nasser's greatest achievement. There is no need to recount the story here. But Britain's exclusion did not bring a full measure of independence to Egypt. For the British Empire was anyway, as it turned out, a passing cloud, dispelled by the quickening breeze of global change, vaporised by the strengthening suns of emerging worlds in Africa and Asia.

The years of Free Officer rule have been dominated by the world rivalry of the new powers that have displaced Britain and struggled with subtler forms of imperialism, to win the outlying and uncommitted peoples of the world to their respective causes, called 'communism' and 'capitalism' but seeming rather to resemble the national interests of the Soviet Union and the United States. Even in these difficult circumstances of a world ground between upper and nether millstones, the Free Officers conceived an image, at least, of true independence for Egypt: a strong Egypt, with an important world role at the heart of the potentially mighty Arab nation; even earlier, some elements of this vision had been glimpsed by the Wafd, as Egypt's demand for representation at Versailles in 1919 shows, or Egypt's initiative in the formation of the Arab League in 1945. But in attempting to bring the image to life, Nasser failed. Indeed, in his last fifteen years of power, Egyptian independence was actually eroded as the country was cajoled and manœuvred into virtual clientage of the Soviet Union, even though the abatement of the cold war in the same period enabled more dextrous leaders in other countries to escape from the dilemmatic world of two major 'power blocs' and to increase scope for non-alignment.

It has to be said that failure in this respect was in part self-inflicted. The ferocity with which Nasser pursued his personal conception of Egyptian interests and asserted Egyptian dignity alienated successively all potential friends except the Soviets, on whom he came to rely for the Aswan Dam project, all military supplies, inferior technological aid, and niggardly economic assistance. After the 1967 war, when Soviet policy in pursuit of détente moved wildly out of phase with Egyptian interests, Egypt found herself obliged to truckle reluctantly to the Russians' commands, trapped in the corner into which she had been painted. Nasser became disillusioned and recalcitrant, striving to reorientate his policy towards reconciliation with America in the last months of his life and replying to President Brezhnev's protests, 'After what you've done to me, I would accept a solution from the Devil himself'.

Two facts had eluded the government until too late: (1) that Egypt's policy over the Palestinian problem could only succeed with

American help, for only America had sufficient power in the Middle East generally and over Israel in particular; (2) that Israel's baffling, staggering success in war and diplomacy alike depended on her friendship with the United States and therefore on continuing Egyptian-American enmity; ironically, by remaining aloof from America, Israel's most unremitting foe was serving Israel's best interests. In 1956 a diplomatic wedge might have been driven between Ben-Gurion and Eisenhower and America riveted to Egypt's side. But Nasser was almost incapable of staatspolitik. He seemed almost to believe it was wrong to act according to expediency. The moment passed. By the end of the 1967 war, a reorientation of Egypt's foreign policy was palpably necessary; but a reorientation with fully satisfactory results was no longer possible.

When President Sadat assumed responsibility for Egyptian affairs, Russia had thus become the target of Egypt's continuing quest for independence, the elimination of all super-power patronage its aim. Sadat, who could not accept 'that a guardian power should manage our own affairs' [Sadat, 1978, 173], combined a general intolerance of such patronage with a particular and growing distaste for Soviet methods. He had felt this in some degree ever since the Suez crisis of 1956, when he could not help but contrast American helpfulness with Russian indifference and concluded that it was 'futile to depend on the Soviet Union' [Ibid 146].

Sadat knew America at first hand from his visit in 1966 as Speaker of the National Assembly. He was aware of the shared experience of Egypt and the United States as nations which had struggled against the British Empire and which traditionally pursued ethically determined policies, uncorrupted by narrow doctrines of the primacy of purely national self-interest. He knew well the arguments from expediency in favour of Egyptian-American rapprochement. Though he embarked on no close understanding with the United States before October 1973, it could be argued that he began tentative soundings in America's direction in his first weeks of power: on October 21st, 1970, he gave an interview to the *New York Times,* saying that 'much could be done if America were not so closely identified with Israel' and that Egypt was 'not in the Soviet camp'.

In the first fifteen months of his presidency, Sadat felt the negative effects of Russian-dominated peonage ever more acutely. Three circumstances, in particular, alerted him to the urgency of the problem. First, he found himself unable, throughout 1971, to get the Soviets to honour their promises to re-equip Egypt's armed forces without political conditions; the 'strings' the Russians attached to the proposed deals threatened to turn Egyptian independence into a self-mocking marionette. Secondly, his initially precarious tenure of office was further unsettled by the plots to unseat him hatched by Ali Sabry and the group of officials and ministers whose attempted coup he thwarted in May: this was certainly a left-inclined and pro-Soviet coterie of men whom Sadat himself denounced as Soviet agents [Sadat, 1978, 224].

Finally, the failure of his proclaimed 'year of decision' stung the president to anger at Russian temporising and obstruction. Sadat had proclaimed 1971 as the year in which a decisive step would be taken one way or another, for war or peace, and the Arab-Israeli problem resolved either in negotiation or in battle; but the Soviet Union, in its own interests, was determined to protract the impasse and above all to avoid a recrudescence of war. Sadat subsequently blamed the Russians solely and wholeheartedly for the lack of progress, though he was obliged to refrain from doing so openly at the time [Sadat, 1978, 227].

A sudden *volte-face* in Egyptian foreign policy was neither possible nor desirable. Politically, at home, the Egyptian people were too thoroughly habituated to the language of Soviet friendship to comprehend a rapid change. The United States, as Israel's guardian angel, was too universally detested. There were too many Soviet sympathisers in the armed forces and administration, especially among those who did not belong to the era of the Free Officers' Movement but who were younger and had risen under Nasser, like Ali Sabry himself, in the years of dependence on Russia. Nor was it advisable to throw away Russian friendship, for what it was worth; *mutatis mutandis,* this would be to repeat Nasser's mistake in rebuffing America: one may sail between Scylla and Charybdis by plotting a course equidistant from both.

Sadat hastened slowly, opening channels of communication with America by his peace initiative of February 1971, continuing to praise Russia and exchange visits with her leaders, completing the Soviet Friendship Treaty negotiations and committing himself to no dramatic gesture while the 'year of decision' still offered some prospects of staying afloat or at least of being salvaged. But, with the foundering of those hopes, it became increasingly clear that there would be no Middle Eastern peace without the preparatory purgation — horrible as it was to contemplate — of another round of fighting. As we have seen, the pressures for renewal of war, both within Egypt and in the general conjunction of events, were mounting irresistibly in 1972.

In May, though Sadat was denouncing America as 'more Israeli than the Israelis' and characterising arguments with Russia as 'differences between friends' [Israeli, 207-18], those arguments could not be concealed. In that month there was pressure from a group of former Free Officers for a 'National Front' — in effect, a break with Russia. A campaign in *Al-Ahram* struck the same chord. Against this background, Sadat had to unleash his dogs of war from their Soviet-held reins; he had to distance himself from the power that restrained Egypt from the struggle. And so in July 1972 he took the step which, more than any other single measure, seemed to mark Egypt's transition from dependence to independence by expelling all Soviet military 'experts' from the country.

This was no diplomatic revolution, like the posturings of European powers as they changed allies like suburban wife-swappers before the Seven Years' War, no change of partners in the diplomatic dance. Egypt remained a friend but not a client of Russia; she made no move, undertook no commitment, towards the United States. The expulsion of the experts was seen by Sadat as a 'patriotic decision' [Sadat, 1978, 287]. Egypt fought the war of October 1973 as, in effect, a genuinely non-aligned state — proving, incidentally, that Egypt did not need to enfeoff herself to either of the international barons to protect herself in a dangerous world. Only gradually has Sadat allowed relations with Russia to deteriorate to the point where disaffection rather than friendship prevails; only in 1976 did he cancel Russia's rights to use Egyptian ports and formally abrogate the Soviet-Egyptian Treaty of Friendship; only in 1977 were Soviet consulates closed. Pro-Soviet elements at home continued to be encompassed by President Sadat's régime even later: not until 1978 did the pro-Soviet General Shazli defect to Libya; not until 1979 was the pro-Soviet United Progressive Party totally eclipsed.

The expulsions of 1972 could not mark a definitive turning-point for a further reason: Sadat must have hoped that his blow would sting the Russians into a more positive and helpful response which would facilitate further co-operation. Indeed, an article by Hasanain Haykal — still a powerful voice, close to the president, at that time — in *Al-Ahram* on October 13th, expressed this hope; time was needed to see whether it would be fulfilled. Moreover, the public was only beginning to know the full extent of Sadat's dissatisfaction with Russia and the reasons for it. The break of '72 had not been preceded by a concerted effort to prepare popular opinion. Only after the event did a full-scale press campaign get under way: on August 7th, 1972, the president briefed news editors to the effect that 'hardly a day has gone by without some quarrel with the Russians...My tongue went dry with arguing with them'. He accused the Soviet Union of encouraging Ali Sabry and explained that he had signed the infamous Friendship Treaty only on the strength of an unfulfilled Russian promise to supply long-awaited Mig 23s.

The president's restiveness with Russia bubbled and steamed for some time, like the contents of a coffee percolator, before being poured out in his public denunciation of the Soviets and abrogation of the Friendship Treaty in March 1976. Meanwhile the threat Russian tutelage posed to Egypt's independence had become a public scandal, thanks to the government's frank (but still private) press briefings and to the impact of Ibrahim Saada's brilliant, conspicuous and popular book, *The Russians are Coming,* which exposed Russian infiltration of Egypt and Soviet attempts to manipulate Arab policy by exerting pressure through arms deals and other aid. Sadat put the reality of the relationship clearly in an interview with *Al-Hawadith* of Beirut on March 20th, 1975 (at about the time of the temporary logjam in Dr Kissinger's second disengagement mission between Egypt and Israel): 'My story with the Soviets is that they want to remain our guardians, but I told them that guardianship is finished.'

The Russian foil was still useful while peace negotiations were delicately balanced: if Russia were excluded from the picture, America might be tempted to substitute her own, equally unwelcome patronage. But by March 1976 Sadat felt sufficiently sure of the momentum of the peace drive to risk an open showdown with Russia. He was, moreover, incensed by Soviet failure to provide spares and supplies for Mig 21s (which he had been driven to seek via India's good offices). Russia's refusal to cancel or reschedule debts was a further blow, and an imprudent one on the Russians' part, since, as *The Economist* had observed on November 10th, 1973, the extent of Egyptian indebtedness to Russia was so vast that it tended to limit the freedom of action of the creditor more than that of the debtor. The abrogation of the Friendship Treaty marked the culmination of the worsening Egyptian-Soviet relations of 1975-76. The process of easing Egypt out of the Russian bear-hug, which had been going on since 1970 or 1971, appeared to have reached a definitive stage.

Thus President Sadat comprehensively cast off Russian moorings. But the danger in his method was that in steering away from port he might list too far to starboard; his critics abroad suggested that he might be trapping himself against a lee shore: a predicament, like that to which Nasser fell victim, of over-reliance on a super-power — in Nasser's case, the Soviet Union, in Sadat's, the United States. For three reasons, however, we may be confident that no such eventuality occurred and that President Sadat brought the quest for Egyptian independence to a successful end. First, the relationship of Sadat's Egypt to the United States was not like that of Nasser's Egypt to Russia. America is a more useful and more disinterested ally; Sadat made this point vividly himself when he explained to an NBC interviewer in 1974 that the joint American-Egyptian operation to clear the Suez Canal prior to its reopening had shown him the 'real face' of the United States, or when he said, in April 1974, that entente with America had wrought a miracle in the direction of peace [Israeli, 513]. Secondly, although the need to conclude the 1979 Peace Treaty with Israel forced Egypt into a position of temporary dependence on America because of the suspension of Arab economic aid, the shake-up of Egypt's relations with the Arab world that has accompanied the entente with America has on the whole been favourable to Egypt's independence; this apparent paradox needs to be explained.

On one level, it is no more 'independent' to be a pawn of the oil-rich than of the arms-rich. As early as his *October Paper* of April, 1974, Sadat was presenting the reality of Arab aid to his people, without illusions, as prompted by 'their national motives and economic wisdom' [Israeli, 486]. Disparity of wealth between Egypt and some of the Arab states whose champion she has been in the past has changed the status Egypt enjoyed in the early days of the Arab League. Purse-strings are too strongly reminiscent of puppet-strings for Egypt's comfort. As Sadat put it, 'If we don't have economic independence, we can't possibly have political independence' [*Arab Report*, 31st July, 1979]. Moreover, the legacy of Nasser's Arab policy has left limiting effects on Egypt which only a showdown with the Arabs could dispel. Nasser aimed at leadership for Egypt in the Arab and Moslem worlds: in effect, this meant *being led* by sources of opinion outside the country, notably by extremists whom Nasser felt obliged to embrace or overtrump in his bid for leadership. Sadat has restored Egyptian independence by defying these. Such considerations explain the spirited response Sadat felt confident to make to the Arab boycott in July, 1979, when he accused other Arab states of doing little to help the Palestinians and trying to keep the Egyptian people 'starving and driving them to panic'; he warned that Egypt would have to reassess future relations with other Arab countries 'very, very cautiously' [*Arab Report*, 5th Sept. 1979].

Finally, Sadat was aided by a world climate more propitious for Egyptian independence than existed in the Nasser era. The decline of global super-power domination, the rise of China, the gradual integration of Western Europe and, above all, the emergence of Egypt's new friends in Africa as the nucleus of a nexus of international relations for Egypt outside the super-powers and the Arab bloc. Even the dislocation of Egypt's relations with the Arabs can only be temporary as the basic community of interest between Egypt and the other moderate states of the League gradually reasserts itself — not even at its height was the boycott complete, with Oman, Sudan and Somalia unruffled in their friendship for Egypt.

In building what we have called real independence for Egypt from super-powers and rich neighbours. Sadat erected an edifice that is likely to last. In 'opening the doors that have been shut in Egypt's face' [Sadat, 1978, 212], he created a basis of firm friendship for the future with western powers; he extended the scope of Egypt's future world role by responding to the opportunities of establishing a new network of relations outside the Arab world in Africa. In July 1975 he told O.A.U. leaders in Uganda of his deep faith 'that our lot is one and so are our interests and the challenges we are facing' [Israeli, 973] and he upheld that principle in action, defying old colonialism in Zimbabwe and Namibia, helping to fight Russian neo-colonialism, especially in Zaïre. Zaïre is of special importance as Egypt's diplomatic bridgehead in the sub-Saharan world: Sadat helped with manpower in 1977 and with training facilities more recently. The results of Sadat's African orientation have been twofold: his African friends stood by him at the O.A.U. in July 1979, against the Arab 'rejectionists'; and much of the basis of America's generous arms deals with Egypt is explained by the need to offset Russian and Cuban interference in the continent.

Relations with Sudan are potentially a further source of reliable friendship for Egypt in future and so of guarantees of continuing Egyptian independence. The Sudanese dimension is inseparable from Sadat's African policy, since Sudan, like Egypt, is a nation at the interface of the Arab and African worlds. Support for Sudan was a consistent feature of Egyptian conduct throughout Sadat's presidency, since the Tripoli charter of November 1970. In supporting President Numairy against the 1971 coup attempt, and airlifting Sudanese contingents home to help the legitimate government, Sadat declared, 'We are one people, of one origin, one blood and one destiny' [Israeli, 1517], and although this is an almost grotesque oversimplification of a complex ethnic, religious and historical patchwork, it contains a kernel of truth which has helped to impel both countries towards co-operation.

The present emphasis is on 'integration' *(takamul),* a co-operative, regionally-centred programme which will gradually lead to the establishment of common institutions. This is a moderate, realistic policy and was characteristic of Sadat's political style. One cannot help but contrast it with Colonel Gaddafy's wild schemes for instantaneous Arab unification. If the programme can contrive to be properly sensitive to Sudan's minorities — Christians, southern Sudanese, and Marxists — and can allay traditional Sudanese reticence towards their dauntingly large and populous northern neighbour, the project could bring great benefits to both partners. Relations with Sudan, as with Africa generally, should complement the real independence which Sadat's conduct of foreign affairs forced for Egypt.

The Pursuit of Peace

The winning of genuine independence, the 'liberation of Egypt's will', is arguably the greatest achievement of Sadat's presidency in the field of foreign relations, but it is as a peacemaker that he is best known in the world; peace with Israel, and the trail he blazed towards comprehensive settlement in the area, are accounted by most people to be Sadat's masterpiece of statesmanship. Indeed, there is much justice in this. For although against the great span of Egypt's history the struggle with Israel seems a small, poor thing compared — say — with the long quest for independence, it has thrown up problems of such baffling complexity, which proved intractable to so many efforts, that Sadat seemed spectacularly courageous to wrestle with them, like an Arab David confronting gigantic problems. And to overcome them appeared, like David's, an astonishing feat, even for prowess allied with right.

In winning genuine independence, Sadat was, as we have seen, helped by circumstances. The winning of peace was, in a fuller sense, his personal triumph. It was achieved *against* the force of circumstances. It was a product of skill unaided by luck. It was perhaps the supreme example of how Sadat was never deterred by the impersonal forces that often seem to govern history, but manœuvred and sometimes managed to impose his own will, his own vision of the future, on the course of events. So adverse were the circumstances in which Sadat launched his successive peace initiatives and at last brought them to fruition, that his success almost embodies his own aphorism, 'Politics is the art of the impossible' [Sadat, 1978, 89].

Sadat's peacemaking has been praised for its pragmatism, and it is true that pragamatism was one among several important ingredients of the President's policy. For example, when launching his first initiative in 1971, Sadat was aware that 'we were being, perhaps for the first time ever, objective and realistic rather than emotional and irrational'; in prising America from unmodified pro-Israeli partisanship into a position from which the super-power could work for peace, Sadat realised that he could not ask the Americans to suspend their special relationship with Israel 'proceeding from an objective, realistic stand' [Sadat, 1978, 219, 304].

But pragmatism unalloyed with principle could never be a sufficient source of policy for a man of Sadat's deep faith and finely tuned morality. Where religion and ethics pointed, moreover, history also seemed to lead — and here again we see the historical bent of Sadat's intellect at work. Peace appealed to him, in short, not just because it was politically viable and practically useful but also, more urgently, because it was religiously compelled and historically noble. Islam is the religion of *jihad*, of the Holy War waged unremittingly for the sake of the faith, but it is no crude warrior-creed — as some westerners believe or purport to believe; Sadat's understanding of Islam belonged to the mystical tradition, in which the *jihad* is internalised and transformed into an inward psychomachia, fought against doubt and lust and petulance and caprice and all the inner demons of one's own evil conscience. We have already seen how much of his language is suffused with the glow of faith; in no context was 'Reconciliation is honourable if you are the one who makes it.' In using a victory as the starting-point of a peace initiative he was re-enacting the policy of Thut-moses III towards the Hyksos in the sixteenth century B.C., an episode to which he liked to allude [Israeli, 1336].

Pragmatism, religion, history — three of the most consistent influences on Sadat's thought — conspired to make his quest for peace consistent. For it is important to realise that underlying all the tactical changes of approach he tried over the last ten years of his life was an unwavering policy of peace. Even the warfare he felt obliged to wage the rolling landscape of Sadat's speech more thickly wooded with religious images than when he was speaking of peace. He talked of the duty of sparing coming generations from suffering for which God will call the war-mongers of the present age to account [Sadat, 1978, 305].

In making the appeals for 'peace with justice' which we think of as characteristic of him, he conceived justice religiously, as based on the equality of all men in the eyes of God. He made his historic speech to the Knesset on the festival of the sacrifice of Abraham, whom Muslims regard as the first Muslim for his submission to *Islam* in the strict sense — the way of God. And of all his speeches, that speech to the Knesset was the most richly overlaid with Islamic allusions, like the thick pile of a rare prayer-rug. As for the influence of Sadat's *storicismo* on his peace-making, this was not simply a matter of recognising the historical nature of the Jewish presence in Israel; he was aware of the pharaonic parallels with his own role: his eirenism is another example of the continuity of Egyptian history, which he was always so anxious to stress. In imposing peace from strength he applied a maxim of Rameses II from the thirteenth century B.C.:

was fought — like all rationally inspired wars — for peace. In particular, of course, the 'October' or 'Ramadan' war of 1973 had to be launched in the circumstances of the day to allow peace negotiations to materialise and to prosper. The paradox must be insisted on. Peace was like a salamander that could only be sought in the fire of war. To put it another way, when the Egyptian troops broke the Bar Lev Line they also broke through a wall of illusion and intransigence behind which peace was confined. As Sadat observed in December 1976, 'the momentum of the peace process began from the October War' [*Arab Report,* 21st January 1977]; in a sense Israel had to be compelled to peace through war [Israeli, 452]. To understand this fully, we must retrace in outline the steps by which peace was approached between Sadat's coming to power and the treaty of 1979.

When Sadat became president in 1970, peace was unattainable for three reasons. First, the 1967 war had humiliated and embittered the whole Arab world and Egypt in particular. A lasting peace cannot be imposed in such conditions. The Egyptian people rebelled against the outcome of the 1967 fighting, just as the Germans did against the disaster of 1918. A renewal of war in the Middle East of the 'seventies was as certain as in the Europe of the 'thirties. Secondly, Israel, though she might have been expected to exploit her position of temporary superiority to launch a peace initiative, felt her own security was better served by a continued state of belligerency. In part, this was because, against a background of bitterness and threats of extermination, she did not trust her neighbours to come to terms or to abide by any agreement that could be made. Then again, it was because the cease-fire lines of 1967 constituted more easily defensible frontiers than any Israel had lived with in the past: in the west, they were sufficient to protect her home territory against deep penetration by any weapons the Egyptians then possessed; in the east, they gave Israel command of the Golan Heights on the Syrian front and a shortened line of defence to man on the Jordanian front. As events subsequently turned out, the 'theory of security' which underlay Israeli thinking on these points proved to be flimsy and short-lived. Over the next ten years, the experience of the October war, the improvements in Egypt's arsenal, and the emergence of a chance of a reliable peace, enshrined in a treaty and protected by guarantees, eroded and displaced it.

But as we recall the problems of '67-'73 we have to forgo the advantages of hindsight to understand how the Israelis felt at the time and why they were reluctant to commit themselves to peace. Sadat likened the 'theory of security' to the old Arab tale of the king's golden clogs or — to use the corresponding western image — the emperor's new clothes, and it is true that in time the theory came to seem as fragile as the royal footwear and as insubstantial as the imperial apparel [Israeli 656]. But this was not apparent to the Israelis until after the October War, at the earliest. The third reason why peace was impossible in the aftermath of 1967 was that, in the absence of any real commitment to peace among the belligerents, only the United States had the power and influence to impose peace; until the October War, however, America was reluctant to exert her strength to coerce or even cajole any party in the conflict. Of course the long-standing problems of the fate of the Palestinian people and the status of Jerusalem remained in 1967, as they remain to this day, insoluble short of some sacrifice of principle by one of the contending parties; but the evidence of the last few years shows that a peace process can begin despite these problems. The particular impediments to peace between 1967 and 1973 were the three factors we have identified: Arab revanchism, Israeli intransigence, American impotence.

Thus a recrudescence of war was virtually inevitable. On the other hand, Sadat realised that Egypt was not yet ready to renew the struggle. In the circumstances he decided to prepare for the further round of fighting that might unlock the door to peace, while at the same time exploring the terrain on which some future process of peace might be built. It was therefore with at best only very long-term expectations that he launched his first peace initiative in February 1971, because — as he candidly admitted — 'military action was ruled out at that time' [Sadat, 1978, 208]. Although the initiative was abortive, it contributed to the achievement of a future peace in one vital respect: it included the promise that Egypt would be prepared to sign a peace agreement with Israel and recognise Israel's right to exist as a sovereign state. This *sine qua non* of a realistic peace had not been admitted on the Arab side before, though the super-powers and United Nations were committed to it; in acknowledging it and sticking to it, Sadat showed typical courage, realism and sincerity — even amid preparations for the ineluctable next round of fighting — in the cause of peace.

The first Sadat peace initiative assured the region of at least eleven months' respite — the 'year of decision' Sadat proclaimed 1971 to be. But, with the year's close, war preparations had perforce to increase in earnestness, urgency, and intensity. The world spent 1972 and most of 1973 in mounting expectation of renewed hostilities. April 1972 found Sadat 'agonising about the time of war...We are patient and we keep silent until we complete our war with Allah's help' [Israeli, 190]. His problem was Egypt's unreadiness — verging on incapacity — for war, exacerbated, as we have seen, by the paucity of military aid from Soviet policy-makers bent at that time at least on a temporary peace. Not only was the economy of Egypt a most unconvincing basis for any war effort; not only was the army deficient in all necessary material; but there was — Sadat revealed — not even any offensive strategic plan, so crabbed and diffident was Egyptian military thinking after 1967. The Egyptian staff were the victims of negative expectations and preconceptions as limiting as those of the French in 1940 — and potentially as disastrous.

Sadat began to change all that with the appointment of General Ismail Ali as Commander-in-Chief on October 30th, 1972, with clear orders to prepare an offensive plan. He tackled the task in a way brilliantly calculated to maximise morale, by asking every front-line officer to contribute ideas. The plan was ready by January 1973. Simultaneously, the home front was being mobilised. Sadat himself formally launched the war effort in a broadcast and televised speech to the People's Assembly on December 28th, 1972, in which a new, purposeful tone was discernible as the president announced (prematurely, in fact) that the military plan was ready and that the preparation for the domestic and diplomatic fronts had begun [Israeli, 289]. By the end of 1972, £95m. had been spent on civil defence preparations [*Arab Report*, 31st January 1973]. All Egypt was abuzz with expectation of the coming 'total confrontation'. It was rumoured that the army had been ordered to adopt a war posture within six months [*Arab Report*, 31st December 1972]. A state verging on martial law was instituted at the cost of the postponement of Sadat's dearly cherished plans for democratisation, as the President took the reins of Prime Ministerial office into his own hands.

The events of the first eight months of 1973 were like a

countdown to war, stones on the 'road to Ramadan'. While making diplomatic soundings, Sadat tricked the enemy — as the Israeli defence minister, Moshe Dayan, later admitted — by rattling sabres ostentatiously in May and August, provoking the Israelis into costly mobilisation and operations and deluding them into a 'cry wolf' mentality that left them immobilised when the real crisis came in October. From June onwards, Sadat was toiling, almost unheard and unseen, behind the scenes. In August and September he was receiving frequent visits from Kamal Adham, King Faisal's adviser. For Saudi support, especially through control of the Arab 'oil weapon' to pressurise Israel's western friends, would be crucial in the war, and Faisal had personally assured Sadat of it. In September, activity was phrenetic: on the first, the Egyptian-Libyan unit plan was salvaged by a new formula for a joint constitutional commission. On the sixth, Sadat addressed the non-aligned nations' conference in Algiers and took the chance of a last rallying of the Arab world into unaccustomed unity. On the twelfth, diplomatic relations with Jordan were resumed. When Sadat said that he would have 'no more talk of war', he deceived his adversaries with a delicious *double entendre:* by the time of that remark, on the anniversary of Nasser's death on September 28th, preparations for war had been completed and the date decided.

Typical of Sadat's preparations was his interview with the Air Force Commander-in-Chief, Husni Mubarak, who was later to become Sadat's Vice-President and successor. Sadat summoned him to Mit Abul-Kum that September and said:

> Listen, my son...I called for you today in order to ask you one question, and I want to hear from you a clear and definite answer. Tell me, my son, is the Air Force ready for the battle or not? Think before you give me an answer. If it is not ready tell me so frankly. Unless you are a million per cent sure, do not say it. We have been struck twice and if the Air Force is struck for the third time, that would be the end of us... [Morsi Saad El-Din in *Cairo Today,* November 1981].

There is no need to recount here the familiar story of the October War or to enter the sterile controversy over the balance of military advantages and disadvantages at its conclusion. For our purposes, what matters is that for Sadat the war was a virtually unqualified success. It fulfilled what he wanted from it. It brought Egypt a sufficient measure of military victory to secure the political objectives which the country entered the war. In addition, it was, in psychological terms, a total victory, which transformed Egypt's reputation in the world, morale at home, and potential power at the conference table. Above all it brought a chance to create the peace which, as we have seen, had always — even in the launching of the war — been the underlying objective of Sadat's policy. A metamorphosis was wrought in Sadat's standing with his people. 'I never before believed in the role of the individual in history,' wrote Youssef Idris in *Al-Ahram,* 'but the hero, Anwar Al-Sadat, is beyond my comprehension.' It was representative of a whole genre of hero-worship.

The president began to prepare a peace initiative even before a cease-fire was mooted. As he told the People's Council on December 16, 1973. 'We have fought for peace'. What a remarkably rapid adjustment this was from a war mentality to a peace mentality, the one demanding total, uncompromising commitment to the struggle, the other requiring equanimity, sensitivity and all the arts of compromise! One cannot help but contrast Sadat's response to victory — an immediate quest for peace — with that of the Israelis in 1967, when they showed no comparable magnanimity in victory. Sadat always publicly attributed his decision to accept a cease-fire on October 19th to the problems posed by American involvement in the war, supplying Israel with a stream of new weapons which impeded Egyptian victory. But it would be disingenuous to deny that the timing of the cease-fire was influenced by the uneven course of the battle and the uncertainties created by Israeli counter-attacks, both on the eastern front and at Deversoir, where Sadat — probably with wishful thinking rather than strategic acumen — likened their breakthrough to the Battle of the Bulge in the Ardennes in 1944. Whatever Sadat thought of the military threat posed by this Israeli manœuvre — and to judge from his public utterances he viewed it with contempt, while the military advice he received in private filled him with apprehension — he was certainly disquieted by it because he feared the Israelis could exploit it psychologically, through their mastery of propaganda and relations with the world's influential Anglophone press, to create a clear impression of Egyptian defeat. He admitted that he worried so much about this danger that it made him physically ill [Sadat, 1978, 270].

The reversal at Deversoir was partly the result of his own strategic interference with his generals. He later admitted that it was he who overruled General Shazli's wish to withdraw forces from the eastern front to resist the Israeli counter-stroke. But he was aiming for a spectacular psychological victory. He could not risk even the semblance of a retreat. Military considerations properly understood were of secondary importance to Sadat. He wanted a quick honourable peace — indeed, Egypt was probably incapable of sustaining the fighting for much longer. Sadat's strategy was at best intuitive, at worst militarily unsound. But it was consistent with his political objectives.

Once the peace process began, Sadat sustained it unflaggingly. His thousand attentions were as essential to its survival as the ministrations of a good nurse to the recovery of an ailing patient. To vary the image, he harried it and worried it, sometimes barked or even snapped at it, like a good sheep-dog hurrying an errant lamb towards the fold. He realised that the participation of the United States was vital and that the success of the October War had created the right conditions for American influence to be brought productively into play. Within a few days of the end of the war he sent Ismail Fahmi to Washington to initiate a joint Egyptian-American request for peace.

At first events unfolded with gratifying rapidity. By November 1973 it was certain that in a sense the October War would pay for itself in hundreds of millions of dollars' worth of increased Arab aid to Egypt. Moreover, Arab unity, symbolised for Sadat by the emotional sobs of the ruler of Kuwait as he enquired by telephone at the height of the October War about the progress of Arab forces, was immeasurably useful in helping to bring pressure to bear on America to stimulate the peace process — an ironical spin-off, since peace was unacceptable to many Arab rulers. The early months of 1974 saw a series of successes for the newly established rapport between Sadat and his 'brother Henry' the U.S. foreign affairs adviser, Dr. Kissinger: the first-stage military disengagement on the eastern front in January, the disengagement in the Golan area in May, and the visit of President Nixon to Cairo in June. Sadat fuelled the process, at the risk of alienating the Russians, by withholding no co-operation from Dr. Kissinger and praising his efforts and those of the American government.

In the following years, when the peace process seemed stymied, Sadat revived it with another of those diplomatic *coups de foudre* at which he was so adept. The first had been his peace initiative of February 1971, the second, the October War; the last was to be his spectacular journey to Jerusalem to salvage peace in 1977: all advanced the cause of peace. The gesture he applied in 1975 was to reopen the Suez Canal. It came on June 5th, on the eve of the anniversary of the terrible war of 1967. Timed with a brilliant sense of theatre it was a calculated risk, as Sadat said, 'for the sake of peace. In search of peace, everything is permissible' [Sadat, 1978, 274].

As he navigated the canal in what he described as 'part of the peace process', he felt touched with a sense of rebirth [Israeli, 908]. The gesture proved well judged in its effects. The Israelis made a unilateral withdrawal from the disengagement lines, and the second stage of disengagement was completed in September. In October the Sinai agreement followed, which assured Egypt of the prospect of recovering some of the Sinai resources, pending the negotiation of a full peace treaty, and bound Israel and Egypt to settle their differences without recourse to war. Sadat himself visited America to a genuinely and deeply sympathetic welcome.

1976 was a disappointing year, a trough of low pressure in the climate of peace. In the summer and autumn Sadat was driven by the lack of progress to disclaim Kissinger's 'step by step' approach and call for a comprehensive peace or nothing. But in some ways this was a siren call, a misleading cry that belied the real course of events which were still maturing over a longer term. The elections of 1976 in Egypt, the United States, and Israel went a long way to account for the pause in the momentum of peace. And Sadat was anxious to reassure his people in Egypt and the public in the wider Arab world that he was true to his own conviction of the need for a peace which included a settlement of the problems of the Palestinian people. Sadat consistently emphasised that the Palestinian question has always been the *casus foederis* in the Middle East and that it must be settled if the cause of war is to be removed, from the commencement of the peace process on October 16, 1973, when he told the People's Council that Egypt had fought 'to find a way to restore and honour the legitimate rights of the Palestinian people' [Israeli, 430], through his visit to the Knesset, whom he addressed frankly on the Palestinians' behalf, to the very text of the Egyptian-Israeli treaty itself where the need for a Palestinian settlement is specified. Sadat remained true to the need, as he said, for a solution of the Palestinian problem before there could be any lasting peace [*Arab Report*, 30th April, 1979].

Although Egyptian public opinion has long been 'Egyptian first and Arab second', neither Sadat nor his people was devoid of Arab sentiment; neither was so politically myopic as to believe the Palestinians can be excluded from the process and benefits of peace. In 1976, in particular, when the Palestine Liberation Organisation had not yet forfeited its esteem in Egyptian eyes, Sadat could not have seemed to slight Palestinian susceptibilities, even had he been temperamentally capable of contemplating such an uncharacteristic tergiversation.

On the other hand, true as Sadat was to his Palestinian loyalties, it must be admitted that the last five years have seen Egyptian ardour cool towards the Palestinian cause. The Egyptian negotiating position — while firm on the principle of Palestinian autonomy — has become estranged from that of the P.L.O. It was this process that freed Sadat's hands and enabled him to revive the faltering peace process late in 1977. The reasons for it are not far to seek: the Palestinians' grudging attitude towards Egyptian help; their alignment with Arab 'rejectionists' who have condemned Egyptian peace-making; and above all, perhaps, the sanguinary methods of terror and assassination which the P.L.O. has not only continued to practise but has turned against fellow Arabs in internecine bloodshed.

Symbolic of the way Egyptian patience has been exhausted and Egyptian fellow-feeling alienated was the Larnaca incident. In the prelude to Larnaca, terrorists of unidentified affiliations but Palestinian sympathies murdered Sadat's friend, the respected Egyptian writer, Yusuf Sabai, Chairman of *Al-Ahram* and Secretary of the Afro-Asian People's Solidarity Organisation; they commandeered an airplane, which spent some time grounded at Larnaca; Egyptian commandos made an unsuccessful attempt to arrest them, in the course of which fifteen Egyptians were killed by Cypriot National Guardsmen, universally believed to have been assisted in their attack on the Egyptians by a Palestinian unit whose presence at the airport has never been fully explained.

Thus Palestinian excesses worked indirectly and ironically for peace. But it required the great initiative which Sadat launched with President Carter in 1977 to generate the momentum that led to a treaty. Sadat has recounted the six stages of this initiative in his book of reminiscenses, *In Search of Identity.* They began with a letter to Sadat from Carter, the contents of which have not yet been made public but which the Egyptian leader regarded as the *fons et origo* of the initiative. Then came the failure of efforts to reconstitute the Geneva peace conference — the long-standing framework for a Middle East peace settlement — by means of a working party: this convinced Sadat that if peace was to have a chance, a new initiative would be necessary. Next came his meeting with President Ceausescu of Romania, who convinced him that the Israelis genuinely wanted peace: Sadat therefore concentrated his inventive powers on devising a new initiative. His next idea was to invite the 'Big Five' to a meeting in Jerusalem, but this seemed impracticable and the outcome unpredictable. At this point, a fifth strand joined the thread of his thought — his desire to perform the Great Bairam prayers in Jerusalem, Islam's House of Holiness, and to visit the occupied Arab land. From this evolved the master-stroke of penetrating and addressing the Knesset, flinging down a challenge to peace which the Israelis would certainly find irresistible and which the world would applaud and support [Sadat, 1978, 304-308].

The journey to Jerusalem was a pilgrimage, a 'truly sacred mission', as Sadat called it [Sadat, 1978, 310], in the second most holy shrine of the Muslim faith. Sadat spoke to the Knesset in a mood of religious exaltation that exactly suited the needs of the moment. It is a famous speech, of transcendental importance not only in the history of the Middle East but also for the study of Sadat and the workings of his mind and heart. It is a text which belongs as much to homiletics as to politics, with its stirring evocation of the common monotheistic heritage of Muslims and Jews, its belief — strongly Islamic but intelligible to Jews and Christians — in the closeness of God's relations with man and human dignity and equality before God. Like a sermon, it is written for a feast day — the feast of the sacrifice of Abraham — and gives the biblical story a vivid immediacy. Sadat's avowal that Abraham, the common patriarch of Muslims and Jews, 'submitted to God's will not out of weakness but out of a great spiritual force' becomes at once an appeal for peace and a vindication of the role of the Egyptian and Israeli peacemakers [Salem-Babikian, 17].

Even after this *tour de force,* a long, hard stretch of country remained to be crossed before the treaty could be signed; it took more than a year to cross it. But we can now see with hindsight that from the day of the Feast of Abraham's Sacrifice the conclusion was never really in doubt. What is remarkable in the recent history of the peace process is the way psychological or moral and economic effects have been generated in Egypt. Psychologically, the Egyptians and Israelis have adjusted quickly to peace. For such old enemies, they have been extraordinarily quick to establish a mutual understanding, exemplified by Sadat's rapport with the crowds on his third visit to Israel in September 1979, or the way Tawfik al-Hakim believes that a common, national basis of co-operation exists between Israel and Egypt.

On May 9th, 1979, *Al-Akhbar* coupled the names of the countries as the 'two civilised parties in the Middle East'. Sadat's friendship with Menachem Begin, the Israeli premier with a reputation for toughness in negotiations, was representative of the two countries' *entente.* The two leaders shared a common past as armed conspirators — each in his own way — against the British Empire. They were therefore able to understand one another in the present. Begin defied his security advisers to walk in the procession at Sadat's funeral out of a genuine depth of personal regard, as well as to preserve the momentum of peace which, if sustained, will be the best monument to Sadat's memory. This suggests that, although the long-term future of the region remains unresolved while the Palestinian question continues to dangle menacingly on a thread of uncertainty, the Egypt-Israel peace treaty will not be lightly discarded. There is every possibility that outstanding differences will be peacefully, even amicably settled. The best course for Arab 'rejectionists', who will be unable to wage war without Egypt's help, may be to accept the peace process and join it in order to accept the best possible terms for the Palestinians. On the other hand, it is hard to see clearly beyond 1982, when the last fragments of occupied Sinai will return to Egypt under the Camp David agreement. If the Israelis have not by then made significant progress towards an accommodation on the Palestinian question, Egypt will no longer have any interest in maintaining the Camp David momentum. The onus is therefore squarely on the Israelis to keep Sadat's initiative alive.

At the end of the day, Sadat was obliged to accept what was tantamount to a separate peace between Egypt and Israel. It would be wrong to suppose either that this was what he wanted all along or that he was tricked into it by President Carter and Mr. Begin. It was a partial solution which he espoused with reluctance. But it was the intransigence of the rejectionist Arabs which forced him into it. By refusing to join the peace process or concede Israel's right to exist, the Arabs left Sadat with no means of furthering the cause of peace save to sign the 1979 treaty, leaving the Palestinian question unabandoned but unresolved. Disunity in the Arab world over the Lebanon, the Iran-Iraq conflict, the price of oil, the super-power balance, the future of the Saharan states, and virtually every other issue on which an Arab consensus is wanted and wanting, has been such that a united front even on the question of peace with Israel has been inaccessible to the best efforts, first of Egypt and, more recently, of Saudi Arabia.

Now, through the Fahd plan, Saudi Arabia has virtually admitted Israel's 'right to exist', causing a further split in the rejectionist camp and making a mockery of moderate Arab unwillingness to support Sadat's initiative. In these circumstances, not only was Egypt justified in seeking her own solution: she had no other choice. To wait for Arab unity would have been to postpone peace indefinitely. Egyptians bore the brunt of all four Arab-Israeli wars. Even after Egyptian forces won the first and only Arab victory over the Israelis in 1973, the other Arabs offered only stinted solidarity and parsimonious aid. If there was another war, it would again be Egypt that would make the biggest sacrifice. Egypt suffered a hundred thousand casualties fighting vicarious battles for Palestine. Hardly a single family has not lost a father or a son or endured some hardship. After experiences like these, it is only right and natural that Egyptians and Israelis should want peace and friendship — like, say, the French and Germans after the comparable series of wars they have waged against each other in recent history. Jihan Sadat expressed the appropriate emotions in a letter to a bereaved Israeli woman:

> In every soldier who fell in the War of the Tenth of Ramadan there is our son and a part of our soul...
> Wars know no real victor, no real vanquished...the price is enormous and painful. It is the sacrifice of thousands of young people, the mourning and grief in the hearts of the

mothers, the wives, the fathers [*The Times,* 15th March 1974].

It would behove Egypt's erstwhile Arab friends to acknowledge not only the wisdom of sentiments like these — conventional wisdom, and no less true for that — but also their inevitability.

Even before the conclusion of the treaty, in 1978, Egypt obtained from America (without counting on-going long-term aid projects or military assistance) an $11 m. irrigation scheme to replace pumping stations in Aswan and Qena and provide seventeen stations in Beni Suef, Al-Minya and Sohag; $26 m. in irrigation and drainage-maintenance equipment; $25 m. for the renovation of Cairo's sewers; $20 m towards the replacement and renewal development plan; $488,000 for health and social services in Menufia; and when longer-term aid programmes are taken into account, Egypt received over $900 m. in U.S. economic aid. In the year of the treaty itself, U.S. economic aid amounted to $1.2 billion. In addition, one must take into account the relief to Egypt's budget granted by American arms aid, the revenues of the reopened Suez Canal ($600 m. in 1979), profits on the recovered Sinai oilfields ($1 billion in 1979), the fillip to tourism, the foreign investment, and the prospect that Cairo will replace beleaguered Beirut as the international financial centre of the Middle East. Social projects have benefited from the release of military manpower and expertise to help with civil construction and engineering.

However the value of peace is reckoned, whether in crude terms of its economic pay-off or in terms of its social, psychological, moral, and diplomatic benefits, it appears to be an impressive source of good for Egypt. The personal contribution Sadat made to its achievement was for him a just cause of proper pride. Enemies are never easy to reconcile, especially in the century of total war, when destructive victories have been relentlessly pursued and unconditional surrenders demanded as a matter of course. Sadat had sufficient statesmanship to step outside this sort of course. He deserved the partial success he achieved.

CHAPTER SIX

Assassination

Towards the end of his life Sadat's success stagnated. The stability of Egypt, which he had constructed so painstakingly, showed increasing signs of strain: the 'momentum', of which he was an exponent and master, seemed in the last year of his life to have deserted him. He died on a downturn. He showed his awareness that he was entering a time of crisis when he became his own Prime Minister in a cabinet reshuffle of May 1980, on the anniversary of the Corrective Revolution. Not since the war of 1973 had he assumed such direct responsibility for coping with a national emergency. It was a public acknowledgement that the circumstances were again perilous. Time was running out for the peace process. Internal unrest was mounting. Yet, considered from a long-term perspective, all was not wormwood. Sadat's greatest schemes were generally slow-maturing by nature and the world had hardly begun to see their results when their creator was gunned down.

For Sadat was a leader who planned ahead. Pride in foresight was a feature of his statesmanship. His economic policies were intended to bear fruit over generations rather than decades. He looked forward, for instance, to a country-wide redistribution of Egypt's population that could only be achieved at best over several lifetimes — a 'desert in bloom' that could only come into being very gradually. His vision of a community of nations at peace throughout the Middle East was a vision for a remote future. Even the sort of detailed economic planning which in most countries is hardly hazarded over a period of five years ahead was, at Sadat's insistence, attempted over a twenty-year term in Egypt. His energy programme, building beyond the usefulness of the Aswan Dam and beyond the lifetime of Egypt's oilfields towards a nuclear- or solar-powered future for coming Egyptian generations, was a dramatic proof of his belief in preparing well ahead to keep pace with accelerating change. So, although he had spent eleven years as president of his country when the assassins killed him, his greatest projects had scarcely begun to ripen. The timing of his death, complained of the lack of investment in livestock and agricultural land reclamation [*MEED,* 9th April 1981]. Finally, a few weeks before his therefore, threatened his reputation. He expected to serve another term at least — his constitutional changes of 1980 showed that. The perspective of his critical, even catastrophic, last year in power is too shallow to judge him by.

Still, it must be acknowledged to have been a dangerous time. It can be argued that the far-sightedness of Sadat's planning was actually a source of weakness in his régime. Democratic governments — such as Sadat aspired to lead — have to work for short-term gains to appease popular demands. The need to impose remoter aspirations on the people compelled Sadat to make occasional lapses from his own democratic standards: to crack down from time to time on the press and broadcasting, to keep opposition parties on a rein, to fix strict limits to the public utterance of criticism. The gap between the rhetoric — indeed, the partial realisation — of democracy and the need to force through policies to which he was committed in the long-term in the face of popular scepticism and short-term sacrifice introduced a note of tension into his relations with his people. Demonstrators in 1977 and 1979, for instance, accused him of neglecting the interests of the poor — an unjust charge, but one which illustrates the extent to which his policies, with their postponed aims, were misunderstood.

The allegation that Sadat never inspired the affection of the poor, as Nasser did, is probably fair — at least as far as the urban poor are concerned. In any period of major economic restructuring they form the class whose problems are most acute and whose benefits longest delayed. In Sadat's last year the subsistence problem was critical: inflation was running at about 25-30 % per annum. In September 1980 beef sales were banned for thirty days to alleviate shortages — and Egypt already had one of the lowest consumption rates of meat and meat products per capita in the world. In February 1981 food subsidies were cut on all but the vital brown pat loaf, while the I.M.F. pressurised the government to make the cuts go further. These food subsidies had become, since the riots of January 1977, the symbol of the régime's understanding with the poor — a kind of criterion of compassion which it was politically impossible to abandon. In April 1981 U.S.A.I.D. admitted the failure of its efforts to boost food production, while the minister responsible, Uthman Ahmad Uthman, death, Sadat learned that over the next five years a food-imports bill of $20 thousand million would have to be met if the people were to be fed.

The incipent crumbling of Sadat's régime was shown in nothing more than the growing opposition in groups among the intelligentsia who had formerly been his most loyal supporters. After all he had done for lawyers and writers, this *trahison des clercs* was particularly hard for him to bear. In some respects its beginnings went back to the New Wafd, which had been particularly strong in lawyers and graduates and for which the eloquence of Fuad Serageddin had procured a generous reception in the Bar Association. Stifled when the New Wafd was disbanded, the intellectual opposition re-emerged in a more militant form in 1980.

In January and February intellectuals began an evidently concerted process against the government's plan — deeply cherished by the president, who was, to a large extent, its author — to set up a court of ethics to guard the moral values which Sadat regarded as hallmarks of Egyptian national identity. The court would be empowered to try anyone who publicly showed disrespect for divine law or offended public feeling. Communists and religious extremists, it is clear, were intended to come within its purlieu. It was important that 'divine' rather than 'Islamic' law was specified, since the court was particularly designed to protect the sensitive Christian—Muslim balance and defend Christians against the blasphemies and brutalities of Muslim fanatics. A new law enshrining the values and ethics Sadat thought essential was being actively projected. The president seems to have been genuinely uncomprehending of the horror this court and this law would be bound to inspire in liberal breasts. A disciplinary tribunal with a window onto men's souls, an inquisition with dangerously vague jurisdiction, a code of values invigorated with the force of law, and — above all — a new potential instrument of tyranny that could easily be perverted to political ends: these were things too horrible to be hallowed even by the best intentions. Abdul-Aziz Shuragi, former president of the Bar Association, warned that every man's freedom could be shackled. Naguib Mahfouz, the ingenious writer whose pen had served Sadat's turn in the past, denounced the government's plans as suppressive of thought and obstructive to culture [*MEED*, 8th Feb 1980].

In spring of that year, the opposition of intellectuals was fuelled by Sadat's new constitutional proposals, toughened by a People's Assembly anxious to show itself *plus royaliste que le roi*. The new constitution would allow Sadat unlimited terms as president and would entrench Egypt's mixed economy, multi-party system, and independent press; it would identify the Islamic Sharia as the basis of the law of the state and create an upper parliamentary chamber called the 'Shura Council' in an effort to impart an air of the sanctity of the Sharia to this essentially secular political body: it was to be composed of elected and presidentially appointed members in the ratio 2:1. The constitution was opposed by all who feared presidential autocracy. The widespread sense — emanating, to some extent, from Sadat himself — that the régime was in decline contributed to a reluctance to see its life protracted by constitutional tinkering. An open letter of protest was signed by fifty-two prominent opposition figures, including some former ministers. Meanwhile, in a darker penumbra of opposition, farther from the centre of authority, in the universities and among disaffected exiles, the communist party was experiencing a revival. In the spring of 1980 thirty suspects were on trial in Cairo for organising the party and twenty men were under investigation for publishing seditious pamphlets abroad.

Further flaws in Sadat's régime were revealed by a curious scandal which rent Egypt in late 1980 and 1981. The affair was provoked by the publication of a volume of reminiscences by Uthman Ahmad Uthman, who had been regarded as one of Sadat's closest associates. Head of the biggest business in Egypt — a vast, monopolistic construction empire — he was the glowing beacon of Egyptian entrepreneurism and virtually the incarnation of the principles of *infitah*. His reputation for personal probity was unmatched — certainly unrivalled in Sadat's entourage. As a cabinet minister he had master-minded the spectacular progress of Egypt's economic infrastructure. The outrage his memoirs caused seemed out of proportion to their content: he trenchantly criticised both government policy and the conduct of the administration during the Nasser years; but by the 'eighties, Nasser's time seemed remote to many Egyptians, most of whom — such was the pace of demographic change — could remember, if at all, it only as children. Uthman made some new revelations about corruption in Nasser's government, but with no attempt personally to vilify the great leader. Nor was the general tone of his criticism out of line with the broad historical revisionism sponsored by the régime and uttered, indeed, by Sadat himself. Yet Uthman's and Sadat's enemies were able to use these mild animadversions against both the president and the minister. It seemed extraordinary that Nasser's ghost could still be conjured with such devastating effect after ten years' sedulous exorcism. Uthman's book became a quarry of hidden meanings for readers determined to find them. It was said that he was implicitly criticising Sadat, who shared responsibility for the actions of early Free Officer governments. His account was even read as a kind of *roman à clef* designed to denounce corruption under Sadat in the guise of an attack on Nasser. Veiled accusations of corruption were made against Sadat and the hitherto respected Uthman themselves [Al-Ahali, 9th June 1982]. The press, which was short of copy, because of tightening government controls, lavished headlines and column-space on this timely issue. The People's Assembly, which (with Sadat in an increasingly autocratic mood) was anxious not to become a cypher, eagerly took up the affair. To the opposition, which was wary of provoking repression by direct attacks on government, the scandal was especially welcome. In parliamentary debate and a public enquiry, Uthman was censured and obliged to resign. Sadat, in his turn, was obliged to accept the resignation and to make gestures of appeasement towards the Nasserists. The outcome of the affair had something of the flavour of the impeachment of a Strafford or a Laud. On Sadat, though he affected disinterest, the effect seems to have been serious. His feelings of insecurity sharpened. His fear of the opposition increased. The new evocation of Nasser's spectre disturbed him. And he began to brood on the need for some spectacular re-assertion of his authority.

The most intractable problem Sadat faced as his death approached, and the most destructive of reputation and self-confidence, was the erosion of his programme of peace. This great pivot of his policies was threatened by the loss of momentum of the Camp David process. Nothing concrete had been achieved for nearly the last two years of negotiations with Israel. Talks on Palestinian autonomy and the status of Jerusalem had never emerged from deadlock. And time was running out: the Camp David accord had set April 1982 as the target date for Israel's final withdrawal from Sinai. It had been assumed that agreement on the outstanding issues would be achieved by then. But Israel's refusal to make concessions made that assumption seem increasingly unrealistic. Prime Minister Begin was personally unsympathetic to compromise over Palestine and Jerusalem; in any case, the precariousness of his parliamentary majority, forcing him to rely on hard-line votes to stay in office, tied his hands. But this intransigence was counter-productive in at least two respects: it impaired the credibility of the Camp David process, which enshrined Israel's best hope of an acceptable settlement; and it weakened the prestige of Sadat, Israel's best friend in the Arab world.

The slow collapse of Camp David can be seen to have begun in May 1980, when the deadline for Palestinian autonomy talks passed without progress. Sadat was at a loss to find some new way to re-activate momentum. He sent Husni Mubarak on a six-nation European tour in September in the hope of generating pressure on Israel for an accommodation. But the mission, while making useful contracts for Mr Mubarak, failed in its main objective. In November he renewed an already rejected offer to Israel to exchange a million cubic metres of Nile water a day for a settlement of the questions of Jerusalem and Palestinian autonomy. Shortly before his death he attempted a 'second pilgrimage of peace' — not, this time, to Jerusalem, but to Europe and America, to revive momentum and urge new initiatives that might supplement the work of Camp David. In August in London he urged the United States to recognise the P.L.O. even without any prior Palestinian commitment to recognise Israel, as a means of stimulating negotiations. But he was perhaps over-optimistic in supposing the Reagan administration capable of initiatives as bold and imaginative as his own.

Meanwhile, as Sadat grew more and more desperate in his search for new sources of stimulation for the flagging peace process, disillusion and opposition built up in Egypt. On February 26th, 1981, members of the Egyptian lawyers' syndicate set fire to the Israeli national flag on the steps of their building. The main opposition party, the Socialist Labour Party, announced the withdrawal of its support for Camp David because of Israel's annexation of East Jerusalem and continuing policy of colonisation of the West Bank of the Jordan. Egypt's national consensus in favour of Sadat's peace policy had broken down. The strain on the régime began towards the end to tell on Sadat in a personal way. He grew increasingly autocratic and suspicious, cocooned in wisps of fraying morale. The deteriorating state of internal security was a constant source of anxiety, as the security forces grew probably to the point where they outnumbered the army [A. Mackie in *MEED*, 11 Sept. 1981], while outrages continued unabated.

The president spent more and more time on his memoirs: the opportunity they presented for introspection and meditation helped him to think. He was falling back on his mystic's trick of withdrawal from a world of perplexity. He tried to fortify flagging morale by wearing even more splendid uniforms — according to the *Sunday Times* of London [11th October 1981] the uniform in which he died, of blue and gold with a sash of sacred green, caused audible gasps from the crowds when it was revealed on the morning of that fateful parade. This was journalistic hyperbole of course, but it made a true point about Sadat's sartorial taste. His love of photography became more egocentric. He liked to have himself snapped in poses and dress that reflected his favourite images — taking exercise, in uniform, in a family setting. He grew intemperate in his table talk: rejectionist leaders were 'pygmies', 'monkeys', 'worms'. Sometimes his frustration overflowed in outbursts given in public interviews. An American T.V. programme presuming to compare him with the Shah in pre-revolutionary Iran drew from him the extraordinary theory that American pressure groups and international Zionism were trying to smear his image and undermine his peace efforts [*Mayo*, 13th July 1981]. The virulence of his reaction shows the depth of the crisis with which he was faced. Only the gravest circumstances could have exhausted Sadat's exceptional resources of inner calm and exposed him to the ordinary impatience of the great man frustrated. For that, in essence, was the root of the delicate state of Sadat's morale towards the end of his life: he was vexed to the limits of endurance by a world intractable to the bigness and boldness of his ambition.

Social unrest and political opposition, however, could have been contained if unallied with religious convulsions. It was religious fanaticism, more than any other single factor, that stalled and thwarted Sadat's work, imperilled his régime, and at last destroyed his life. Islam looks solid from a distance but is riven by deep and narrow cracks into hundreds of sects and factions. Most of the 1,500 religious associations in Egypt represent the highly coloured spectrum of Islam. It is a religion peculiarly conducive — when properly understood — to social harmony and stability. But it is also peculiarly prone to fundamentalism and fanaticism. Like the Christianity of radical Protestants, it is founded on the unquestionable authority of a single book. And the reader of the Quran, as of the Bible, can, if he is so disposed, find bloodshed and intolerance in what to a literal mind seems the plain and obvious meaning of the text. The comfortable obfuscations of a *sensus catholicus* are unavailable to Islamic fundamentalists and unwanted by them.

The Islamic renaissance of recent years, which has done the world much good, has therefore also, less felicitously, encouraged the fanatics and swollen their numbers. A destructive form of Islamic revivalism has grown with — and, in some respects, outgrown — the constructive form. The renaissance has enriched civilisation, for instance, through modern Egyptian literature and art — 'vital, abundant and dynamic as in the time of the Pharaohs', according to one shrewd observer [Halim El-Dabh, 1981, 15]. Islamic extremism has grown steadily and inexorably in Egypt since the Second World War, without deeply penetrating the intelligentsia, government, and army until recently. It has generated three flashpoints of danger: popular sectarian violence; revolutionary cells and religious murder squads; and the infiltration of secular politics. The first of these has got progressively more difficult to contain, largely because the bigots have to hand an ideal base for their hatred in the form of the Jews and the large, prosperous Coptic Christian Egyptian minority. The world context of religious wars between Christians and Muslims in recent years — in, for example, Biafra, Lebanon, South Sudan, Uganda, and the Philippines — has exacerbated the tension.

In Egypt, the economic grievances of the majority against the relatively prosperous and frequently bourgeois Copts have added to the political dangers. And the Copts' own esteem for martyrdom and susceptibility to revivalism in a beleaguered atmosphere, especially under the forceful leadership of Pope Shenouda, have only made matters worse. It looked as though Sadat was winning his campaign for internal peace until 1980, when enmity between Muslims and Copts, previously confined to minor incidents, could no longer be contained. A gradually worsening series of incidents followed — outrages against priests, violations of Coptic worship, destruction of churches, including some of the most ancient, numinous, and beautiful monuments of Egyptian civilisation. The time-table of violence makes the increasing depth of the crisis clear.

Early in 1980 two bombs shattered the Alexandrian churches of Gait Ainna and Marie Girgis. Mustapha Al-Maghrabi, the presumed leader of Al-Jihad, one of the most ruthless terrorist organisations among Islamic extremists, was killed in an ensuing gun battle. But before dying of his wounds, he confessed to membership of another fanaticist terror group, Takfir wal-higra (to these terrorist cells we shall return in a moment). Seventy members of Al-Jihad were rounded up at once. By the end of January there had been several hundred follow-up arrests; and in a separate operation in Upper Egypt some 1,500 people were taken into custody for a variety of offences including — very prominently — unlawful possession of firearms. The wave of arrests, which touched no important individuals, attracted far less media coverage in the west than a smaller purge in September 1981, when some V.I.P.s were arrested. Despite the government's show of strength, the fanatics replied on January 31st by burning a cinema at which a film about Christ was showing. By April the number of bombed and burned-out churches had risen to six. The Copts called for a Coptic—Muslim committee to investigate the outrages. The Coptic synod complained at violence against Copts, destruction of churches, and forcible marriages of Copt girls to Muslims. Pope Shenouda cancelled Coptic Easter celebrations in protest, only to be warned by Sadat to 'stop playing politics', while Copts and Muslims clashed in Assiut and Minya with many deaths. In June a grenade explosion at a Coptic wedding party in the Cairo suburb of Zawya Al-Hamra sparked off fighting in which there were 10 deaths, 54 woundings, and 113 arrests. The extremist Muslim magazine *Al-Dawaa* ('The Call', run by members of the Ikhwan) had twice to be suppressed in July and August because of incitements to violence. Also in August, the bombing of a Coptic church in Cairo's Shubra district caused two fatalities and fifty-six injuries.

Sadat was bound by his duty as president of both religious communities in Egypt to act to restrain fomenters of violence. His task was made doubly urgent by more general threats to order posed by Islamic extremists. The whole course of his government was anathema to these fanatics — not only or even primarily the peace treaty with Israel but more broadly the attempt to reform society, modernise and humanise the system of justice, emancipate women, and increase the individual's freedom under the law to exercise his own moral judgement. These policies were almost literally diabolical to upholders of Quranic justice, the purdah, and the ferocity of the traditional moral code.

In Iran today alcoholics are proscribed, adulterers stoned, sodomists butchered, thieves maimed, and wives virtually immured. There are Egyptians who admire these excesses and would fight to bring them to Egypt. Sadat's position in these matters was moderate. He was no secularist. By western standards indeed he was a legislative Puritan, who insisted that Egyptian laws be compatible with the Sharia and Islamic tradition, who referred cases of doubt to the learned arbitration of Al-Azhar, and who introduced restrictions on the consumption of alcohol and immodest entertainments. The demands of the fanatics filled him with healthy alarm. His reaction, however, was inadequate to meet the danger. The growth of Islamic fundamentalism in Egypt today is as inevitable as any historical process can be. It is a tide which no Canute can bid recede. Sadat's call for a separation of religion and politics, made in desperation in his last twelve months of life, was simply unrealistic. It ran counter to the profoundly religious inspiration which we have detected at the heart of his own political life. It was incompatible with the dual nature of Islam as a religion and a way of life which are inseparably combined. And the policy announced in the month before his death of nationalising — that is, bringing within government patronage and control — the 40,000 private mosques in which Islamic fundamentalism was preached was far beyond the government's resources.

The desperation of Sadat's proposed remedies reflects the intractability of the problem. It would have been as realistic for Julian the Apostate to suppress the Christians or Charles I the Puritans as for Sadat to contain the fundamentalists. Yet the rise of militant Islam might have been tolerable had its only targets been the Christians and the Law. The proliferation of sects or groups resolved to effect Islamic revolution by violence, however, posed a threat which could be neither avoided nor absorbed. These groups were dedicated to confrontation with the government and to operating outside the available framework of institutions, through terrorism and assassination. Spawned ironically from within Sadat's old confraternity, the Muslim Brotherhood, organisations like Al-Jihad or Takfir wal-higra kept alive a long Islamic tradition of sanctified murder. It was in Islam, after all, that the doctrine of political assassination originated and it is from the medieval Ishmaelite sect of the Assassins that the English word is derived.

But if the ideology of the extremist hit-squads was antiquated, their methods were modern. Their terrorist cells and cadres could enjoy the most up-to-date training methods in Libya or among the P.L.O. Several cells were dedicated to the assassination of Sadat. Beyond the terror cells, lay larger organisations, numerous, over-lapping, kaleidoscopic. The differences of ideology between them were often apparent only to a small group of leaders: rank-and-file membership was much less sharply defined. Members might drift across shifting frontiers from one organisation to another and belong to more than one. Since Sadat's death, study of the organisations has intensified and this has perhaps made them seem less fluid and more coherently structured than they were in reality. In detention, where they were examined, interviewed and tried, terrorists tended to develop their self-perceptions and perceptions of each other. Despite the distortions thus introduced into the record, three important groups are distinguishable in the growth of Islamic radicalism which contributed to the momentum of violence that culminated in Sadat's death. Two of these, known as the Islamic Liberation Organisation (or 'Technical Military Academy Group') and Takfir wal-higra were the subject of a research project led by Saad Eddin Ibrahim, who interviewed detained members over many months after the police round-up of agitators in 1977 [Ibrahim, 1980 and 1982]. Further facts about Takfir wal-higra have emerged since Sadat's death in the Egyptian press as a result of a series of colloquia held in the summer of 1982 between imprisoned adherents of the faction and visiting clergy and journalists [*Al-Liwa al-Islami*, June 1982]. About the third group, Al-Jihad, from which Sadat's death squad appears to have been directly drawn, some information emerged from the assassins' trial: though the trial was conducted in secret, a transcript has appeared in Egypt, with controlled circulation.

The ideological nuances which divide these groups are as

recondite and pedantic as the schisms of primitive Christiantity or the quasi-theology of the early Communist Internationals. They are often imperceptible to the uninitiated, and, in practice, as we have suggested, the membership of all groups probably tended in the past to be fluid and to overlap. All have something of their background in common. All have roots in the old Muslim Brotherhood to which Sadat himself was once affiliated. All began in the aftermath of the terrible introspection and mood of breast-beating that followed the defeat of 1967. All have a strongly corporative flavour, stressing the values of the *umma* — the collective congregation of the faithful — above those of the individual or the family. All throve in the universities in the '70s. All benefited from the indulgence — a fatal, ironically fatal indulgence, as it has turned out — of Sadat's régime from 1970 to 1973, when the president was still hoping to harness the Islamic revival for his own purpose.

The Technical Military Academy Group was the first to achieve public notoriety as a result of a failed coup attempt in 1974. Founded by the young Palestinian-born Salih Siriyya, it was conceived by its members as a development of the tradition of the Muslim Brotherhood. Indeed, the group seems to have coalesced as the result of an approach to 'older members of the Muslim Brotherhood', who merely told the young postulants to 'stay out of trouble and worship God' [Ibrahim, 1982, 10]. The result was a schism: the 'Islamic Liberation Organisation' became a splinter group, but it continued to revere the saints and heroes of the Brethren, especially Hassan al-Banna himself. It was committed to a more active path of Islamic militancy than the now quiescent Brotherhood, but as a potential terrorist leader Siriyya was a relatively cautious man, who wished to postpone an insurrection and renounce symbolic violence. At the same time he tried to give his group a democratic structure and collective decision-making; against Siriyya's wishes, a majority of the collective leadership forced the group into premature action in 1974. Defeat discredited the group's relatively moderate ideology within the fraternity of Islamic radicals. The Liberation Organisation represented Egyptian society not as irremediably corrupted, but merely temporarily diverted from Islamic paths by worldly politicians. Its violence was intended to be directed against the state; random terrorism was rejected. With the failure of Siriyya and his friends, the initiative among Islamic militants passed to the more volatile and extremist organisations, Al-Jihad and Takfir wal-higra, with their commitment to unrestrained terrorism.

The philosophy of Takfir wal-higra is admirably summarised in its name, which, like most pertinent names, probably began as a nickname bestowed by outsiders. *Takfir* is the act of identifying and denouncing people and things that are profane, infidel, or heretical — in a word, un-Islamic. *Higra* is the act of withdrawal from society and, in particular, the withdrawal of the prophet Muhammad from the merchant communities among whom he grew up but who failed to acknowledge his message from God. Takfir wal-higra, then, repudiates Egyptian society as a whole, not just the institutions of the state, and proclaims its own spiritual *apartheid.* Its members withdraw to fight from outside society, like the hermits who thronged the Egyptian desert 1,500 years ago — only, this time, not against demons but foes of flesh and blood. They transform the psychomachia into a real war. They are surprisingly numerous, reckoned at 3,000 to 5,000 in the late '70s, recruited by the operations of kinship, friendship, and worship, members being drawn in gradually by recruiting cadres who slowly, over a fairly long acquaintance, explore and persuade.

The group was founded by Ahmad Shukri Mustapha, a middle-class graduate in his early 30s, while he was in prison for membership of the Muslim Brotherhood, whose work (impeded by repression) he wanted to renew in greater secrecy and militancy. Gaol was the ideal environment — itself a kind of embodiment or shrine of *higra* — in which to identify like-minded men and foster an organisation. Its spread seems to have been strongest among relatively prosperous and educated strata — but that may be a trick of the evidence, reflecting more the social background of the leaders, who tend to end up in gaol. Certainly its appeal is greatest to the young. Nearly all Saad Eddin Ibrahim's interviewees were in their late teens or early twenties.

These tweeny terrorists with their bizarre beliefs have all the explosive confidence of young idealism. They reject the moderating influence of the clergy, much as the I.R.A. ignore the priesthood, but with greater vehemence. They see the Islamic establishment in Egypt as part of the society they reject. Indeed, in 1977 they murdered the former religious affairs minister, Shaikh Muhammad Dhahabi. They denounce the *uluma,* the learned interpreters of the prophet's precepts, as 'parrots of the pulpit'. They are not susceptible to influence from any quarter of authority. And like most political utopians, they have little notion of how their ideals are to be realised in practice. Their vision of the future includes a blurred horizon. How a society on the Quranic model can be constructed from 20th-century starting-points; how literally should the Sharia be interpreted; what is to be done about problems and relationships which the Islamic scripture does not cover; how far the lives and liberty of non-Muslims and moderate Muslims are to be respected in their Utopia: these are problems they have not agreed on, and seem hardly to have discussed. Their vagueness makes them all the more dangerous. Together with the other fanatical factions, they constitute a threat too big and determined to be countered by repression.

The bridge between the background of Islamic militancy and the assassination of Sadat was formed by the organisation known as Al-Jihad. The twenty-four culprits tried for Sadat's murder were welded into a conspiracy by the ideologue of Al-Jihad, Abd al-Salam Farag. He was the author of a rambling and highly derivative tract which became the assassins' vademecum. Entitled by its author 'The Neglect of Duty' it circulated only in manuscript until Sadat's death brought notoriety to its author, when it was published in *Al-Ahrar* as *The Terrorists' Charter [Al-Ahrar,* 14th December 1981]. The argument of this work — if there is one — is inscrutable but the main points are the denunciation of Egypt as an apostate nation, the condemnation of the neglect of fundamental Muslim observance in Egypt, and an insistence that the 'Holy War', literally understood as implying violence and bloodshed, is a 'pillar of Islam', as important as prayer, alms, pilgrimage, fasting and the acknowledgement of Muhammad as the Prophet of God. By comparison with that of Siriyya and Mustapha, Farag's thought seems crude and naive. This perhaps makes it the most dangerous of the terrorist ideologies. Farag seems to owe little to the intellectual progenitor of much Islamic terrorism in Egypt, Sayyid Qtub, whose *Signs along the Road* — a 'work of subversion' as Nasser once dubbed it — declared Egypt to be in a state of *jahiliyya,* the godless chaos of Arabia before Muhammad. In one respect, Al-Jihad was more moderate than Takfir wal-higra: its members did not reject the whole of post-Quranic tradition. In practice, however, they paid it little heed and despised the Egyptian Islamic establishment. Nor did they practise the 'withdrawal from the world' advocated by Takfir wal-higra. This, of course, only made them more dangerous.

Sectarian violence and secular opposition mounted by the summer of 1981 to the point where Sadat, his morale weakened by growing apprehension, felt compelled to react decisively. He cancelled all enagements for the week ending August 28th in order to study the evidence of sectarian violence: this was the period of isolated reflection which characteristically preceded all Sadat's big decisions. At the end of it, he re-enacted with greater ostentation the sort of extensive round-up of subversives last attempted in January 1980. This time he proclaimed it to the world, with a kind of perverse pride, as a 'purge' and an 'electric shock', presumably in the hope of impressing outsiders with the strength of his authority. In fact, however, the arrest of 1,563 opponents of his régime was generally interpreted in the world's media as a sign of weakness rather than power, despair rather than determination. Overwhelmingly, it was Muslim fanatics who were arrested: they were the greatest menace to Sadat personally and public order generally. But there were others included in the purge. Prominent Copts were detained on the ground that their activities constituted an incitement to violence. Pope Shenouda, for instance, was exiled to the sequestered remoteness of a rural monastery and a committee of five bishops was set up to exercise the patriarchate in his absence. This token strike against the Copts was liable to interpretation as a gesture intended to conciliate the Muslims.

At the same time Sadat seemed to be directing blows against personal and political enemies under the guise of relieving sectarian strife. Hasanain Haykal, Sadat's sometime friend and latter-day foe, was arrested and publicly accused of atheism. His reputation as a writer and journalist ensured that this would be ill received in the world at large as a vindictive act of arbitrary authoritarianism. Fuad Seraggedin, whom Sadat had never forgiven for starting the New Wafd, was another victim of the round-up whose fate evoked protests from abroad. The purge had the opposite of its intended effect. Sadat's grip was claimed to be slipping. And for every terrorist, underground leader, and subversive arrested, others were waiting in the capacious ranks of the extremist organisations to take their place.

Sadat was already an accustomed target of assassins by the time of his death. In October 1972 it was reported in Lebanon, though denied in Egypt, that the president had been shot at. In 1974 Islamic extremists attempted a coup in which the killing of Sadat was planned, even though the president was then the hero of the Arab world after the successes of the October War of the previous year. In March 1980 the Chief of Staff, Lt. General Ahmad Baddawi, was killed in a helicopter crash, presumed in some quarters to have been caused by sabotage. The following month Sadat's airplane was diverted from Lisbon to London after reports that a Libyan murder squad was lying in wait. A Palestinian armed with a bomb was thwarted in an attempt to kill the president a few days later. Sadat's cancellation of an intended visit to Austria in August 1980 provoked informed speculation about another possible attempt. And while the régime decayed the plot was thickening in an insoluble whodunit of which Sadat's murder was the climax. It is best to start with what is known: the inferences and hypotheses can be discussed but not resolved. It will be years hence — if ever — that we shall know the full results of the Egyptian authorities' investigation of the conspiracy. But we can start from what little they have so far divulged and from the evidence of the T.V. cameras that recorded the assassination as it happened.

The murder squad was formed by Abd al-Salam Farag and led by a lieutenant of artillery named Khalid Hassan Shafiq Islambuli. He was of impeccably fanatical antecedents. His brother had twice been in prison for suspected association with terrorism and had belonged to the Military Academy Group. 'Shafiq' (as he called himself) had concealed the relationship from his supervisors. He evidently shared his brother's ideals. He formed his murder squad with unerring judgement. The numbers he recruited are unknown but his brother was among them. So were three men who eventually joined him in the actual assassination: an army reservist and two disaffected ex-soldiers who had been discharged with ignominy for defying army regulations on conscientious grounds. These men apparently came together through the extremist underground network of Al-Jihad and Takfir wal-higra. Islambuli's religious grounds for hating Sadat were reinforced by resentment at his brother's imprisonment, which inspired him to comfort his mother with the words, 'Patience. It is Allah's will. Every tyrant must meet his death' [*Al-Ahrar*, 26th October 1981].

The assassins' initial plans must have been flexible and opportunistic, but they certainly included the possibility of an assault.

They trained long and hard, acquiring a level of precision and preparedness that would be vital on the day. They lost the services of Khalid Shafiq's brother when he was rounded up and imprisoned in Sadat's purge, but continued with their plans, until the great parade of October 6th, 1981, at Cairo created the first chance to put them into effect.

Ironically, the date was, by the Roman calendar, the anniversary of the Suez crossing of 1973 which the parade was intended to commemorate, and, by the Islamic calendar, the anniversary of Sadat's first mission to Jerusalem. But there is no evidence that the day had any special significance for the assassins, except as an opportunity to execute their task. Khalid Shafiq had to find a way to infiltrate his squad into the parade, get them close to the president, and choose a propitious moment for the assault of the podium. As far as we know everything went according to plan. On the very morning of the parade Khalid Shafiq sent home three of the men in his artillery unit and replaced them with his gunmen — the two ex-soldiers and the reservist. They smuggled grenades, live ammunition, and sub-machine guns into the vehicle Khalid's unit was to occupy during the parade. No other soldiers taking part had been issued with ammunition and it was absolutely contrary to orders to carry any. But no serious check seems to have been made.

It is not clear how they came to occupy a vehicle that was due to pass close to the presidential podium. It may have been luck, for it was not absolutely essential to their plans; it may have been skill on Khalid's part; it may have been the complicity of a superior officer. But by one means or another they set out at around nine in the morning on a four-hour ride that would bring them to their target. It must have been a nerve-racking drive. The big Russian truck moved slowly at the best of times. Parade-ground pace must have seemed unbearably slow. And there were four regular artillerymen aboard who were not party to the plot. They were unarmed and could be dealt with easily, if necessary, when the time came. But they represented an inevitable and no doubt worrying weakness in the killers' plans.

The set-up at and around the presidential reviewing stand favoured the attackers in many ways. First, no one anticipated an assault from the parade-ground side: all the armed guards were posted for crowd surveillance. Secondly, the stretch of ground immediately in front of the president, which the assassins would have to cross, was out of most guards' field of fire. Thirdly, the president was effectively pinioned to his exposed position at the front of the stand by the dense cluster of V.I.P.s with which he was surrounded: space for flight or concealment was negligible. Fourthly, there was only one security man close enough to the president to try to protect him bodily during the attack. Fifthly, Sadat was unprotected by any kind of bullet-proof garment. It is doubtful whether such a precaution would have been enough against the thorough and determined onslaught he faced, but it is at least possible that it might have made a vital difference. He had sometimes worn bullet-proof clothing on previous occasions. His wife incessantly urged him to do so. But some heroic scruple, some vain-glorious bravado, some deep-seated hubris restrained him: he despised every form of cowardice and was bad at distinguishing what was craven from what was merely cautious.

In the event, the attack succeeded more by surprise than by any other single factor. At first, everyone was disbelieving, then shocked, then numb. The thirty seconds clear in which the killers could operate before any effective counter-action was taken, the forty-five seconds they enjoyed before being gunned down in their turn, were fatal seconds for Sadat. The element of surprise was greatly increased by the fact that the start of the attack coincided with an aerial display by Egyptian Air Force Mirage fighters and other aircraft. For precious seconds, the eyes of everyone on the reviewing-stand were turned skywards. The last photographs to portray Sadat alive show him with gaze uplifted in satisfaction at his pilots' aerobatics.

Death came at the end of a wearisome morning. The president's guests had sat sweltering with him in the crowded stand for an hour and a half, the merciless sun penetrating hot uniforms and uncomfortable best clothes, while the tedious cavalcade rolled past — ten miles of bands and troops and mechanised weaponry, 10,000 men — dragging its slow length along. Ironically, the pace of the funeral procession in the same spot the following week would be rather brisker. The images of the earlier part of the morning had been equally torpid: Quranic recitative, speeches, the president's procession to the tomb of the unknown soldier. The thermometer reached 93 degrees. At noon a display by free-fall parachutists had enlivened proceedings.

The march-past of the Camel Corps added a little local colour. The Mirages' display came as a welcome distraction as the most boring part of the parade — the truck-drawn artillery units that contained Khalid's death squad — lumbered by. It was essentially uninteresting that one lorry should have appeared to break down just in front of the reviewing-stand. Breakdowns were a regular occurrence. The next lorry simply drove round and carried on. Outside, no one knew that in the cab Khalid was holding his machine pistol at the driver's head, forcing him to halt. The four unarmed and innocent occupants of the lorry scattered and fled as the assassins descended, giving the impression to some onlookers that the death squad was more numerous. As Khalid ran, stooped in the assault position, screaming "Glory to Egypt!", towards the president, no one grasped the enormity of what was happening. Many onlookers thought it was all part of the show. The earlier daredevil demonstration by parachutists perhaps disposed people to expect more 'action' entertainment. The stun grenades hurled by the assailants proved ineffective, but the numbing shock of surprise more than compensated.

No one knows why, as the gunmen opened fire, Sadat rose from his seat, presenting a perfect target. Most observers assumed that he thought his attackers were advancing to salute him, and rose in acknowledgement. This is almost certainly false. He can have been in no doubt of their intentions: the posture of attack, the grenades, the way they were positioned — two men held back providing covering fire, two racing ahead, shooting from the hip — made the murderous truth obvious. Moreover, the president's personal guard, Fawzi Abdul Hafiz, was trying to restrain him from rising, though to no avail, and even attempted to cover him bodily with his chair. The best recourse in the circumstances was to fling oneself to the floor, as far as the confined space of the reviewing-stand permitted. Those who managed to do so survived. But that was just the kind of gesture Sadat's characteristic hubris rejected. The likelihood is, as Fuad Muhiaddin suggested in the People's Assembly the following day, that he stood up in defiance, like Napoleon on the Grenoble road but with less happy results. He died with a last act of reckless courage typical of his whole life.

It is not clear at what point during the attack the fatal wound was sustained. The gunmen sprayed the whole reviewing-stand and surrounding area with bullets. People were hit not only in the president's immediate vicinity but also at both extremities of the podium, presumably by stray shots from the death squad's covering fire. But there is no doubt that the killers' main salvoes were trained and concentrated on Sadat in person. The assassins seemed to have aimed not at mass murder but the 'execution' of a single man. They had time to reach the edge of the reviewing-stand, hoist their sub-machine guns over the lip and pump bullets into the space behind, where Sadat's wounded body presumably lay, for four or five seconds before the tardy but intense cross-fire of the guards first drove them back and then cut them down.

Religious zeal can have been the murderers' only motive. Theirs was a suicidal mission, such as only a religious fanatic would undertake. In the absence of any earthly incentive, they must have been inspired, like the Assassins' sect of the Middle Ages, by the hope of rewards in paradise. They were neo-Thuggee, servants of a bloodthirsty deity. At their trial, consistently with the ideology of Al-Jihad, they appealed in their defence to the traditional Islamic doctrines of sanctified tyrannicide. Whether they were also consciously serving the ends of a terrestrial power too is a matter for speculation. Hit-squads pullulate in Middle Eastern politics. It is a part of the world where they seem to kill a leader from time to time *pour encourager les autres*. Sadat's enemies — Gaddafy, Khomeini, and the P.L.O. — are all believed to employ assassination regularly as a political device. All advocate and encourage it. All had threatened Sadat specifically. Colonel Gaddafy, in particular, was suspiciously well informed, at an early hour, of the circumstances and details of Sadat's death, which were crowed over disgustingly on Libyan radio. He had often said — recently, for instance, in June 1980 — that he would support a coup in Egypt and called on his soldiers to 'turn their weapons against Egypt', but neither of these conditions seems to have applied to the murder of Sadat which was planned in conjunction with neither a *putsch* nor an invasion. Gaddafy's protégé, the Egyptian defector, General Shazli, hinted strongly that he had a claim to the tarnished kudos of responsibility for the killing.

But there is no hard evidence to link the murder with any international conspiracy. And the Egyptian authorities have been unwavering in their insistence that interrogation of the assassins revealed no such dimension. Of course, within Egypt, the conspiracy must have been wider than the immediate circle of the twenty-four assassins. The plotters may have hoped that it would trigger off an Islamic revolution, overtrumping the Iranian model, in Egypt. The violence that broke out in the provincial fundamentalist stronghold of Assiut shortly after Sadat's death showed every sign of orchestration: Takfir members in stolen police uniforms launched it by occupying public buildings. But if it was intended as the start of a general insurrection, none ever materialised.

At the scene of the crime it took a long time to mop up the blood. Hours after the murder people were still wandering aimlessly around. Meanwhile the president — flown out with the other victims by helicopter within a minute of the shooting — was dying in hospital. The interrogation of the wounded assassins was under way. The constitutional machinery was clicking into place. At first Cairo Radio concealed the gravity of Sadat's condition, but the news leaked out in the tears of the nurses who attended him and the stoical grief of Jihan, whose return home from the hospital was seen as confirming the rumours of her husband's death. A state of emergency was proclaimed in case the news should spark off disorders or adventurism by the Libyans. The People's Assembly was summoned for the next day to pay its respects to the departed leader and nominate Vice-President Husni Mubarak to succeed him.

In fact, disorder was minimal. Cairo was still thronged with shoppers even as Sadat expired. Thereafter, most towns were silent and the thoroughfares empty. There was no ripple of dissent in the army or security forces. Only in the always febrile university town of Assiut did Islamic fundamentalists take to the streets in a wave of violent release, which lasted some days but was repressed with little bloodshed. Gaddafy tried to incite an uprising from a safe distance over the radio waves but made no attempt to invade. The assassination, as the American Secretary of State, Alexander Haig, said, was simply an assassination, not part of a coup, not an act of incipient war. The state of shock, which began when the shooting started, seemed to spread with paralysing effect through most of Egypt in the next few days. It was sustained through the curiously cold and passionless funeral for which leaders from eighty countries assembled, insulated by an impenetrable screen of security and almost unechoed in any public display of popular grief.

No sooner had Sadat's blood-drenched body been carried from the reviewing-stand than the theory sprang up that 'Camp David had killed him' — that enemies of the peace process had put him to death and that the faltering momentum of negotiations had created a climate of failure which made him vulnerable to conspiracy. There is probably little merit in this theory. Under interrogation, the assassins revealed slight interest in Camp David: their objections to what Sadat represented were more fundamental and more general. Peace, even when his popularity was waning, was the most popular of Sadat's policies in Egypt. But it is true that peace negotiations were stymied at the moment of Sadat's death — so densely stymied, in fact, that only some drastic event, like the president's assassination, could get them going again. In that respect his death was an unwilling but probably effective sacrifice: it transferred responsibility for procuring peace unmistakably to the Reagan administration, which alone could realistically attempt it. Sadat died as he had lived — in a great theatrical *coup de foudre* that generated 'momentum' for peace, just as his 'heroic crossing', his pilgrimage to Jerusalem and his reopening of the Suez Canal, had done before.

Conclusion

The death of a remarkable statesman, once the vaporisings of the obituarists have been dispelled, is an occasion for the release of clouds of venom from his enemies. Nowadays these are instantly transformed into print in the form of pseudo-scholarly or journalistic 'reappraisals'. Anyone who enjoys an outstanding reputation in his lifetime, however well deserved, can expect to be vilified when he dies. In Sadat's case the exultations of his enemies were of indecent proportions. The Arab world held a kind of black wake over his dead body. Libyans took to the streets in an immoderate display of joy. Syrians crowed. Lebanese leftists ullulated. The P.L.O. triumphed. Journalistic buzzards gathered over his bones to make a fast dollar by blackening his memory or settle old scores. *De mortuis nil nisi malum.*

Sadat's reputation can survive this onslaught. For the foreseeable future, the political interests of the western world will alone be enough to ensure that he has defenders in every generation. While Soviet imperialism and Islamic revolutions remain threats to world peace, Sadat will have admirers in the camps he befriended. But, considered objectively, his own work includes enough that was admirable to generate honest praise. As we have seen, even in the domestic sphere, where his talents were smallest and his difficulties most intractable, Egyptians will long have cause to be grateful to Sadat. In foreign affairs, his achievements can be explained away by determined detractors as accidents or illusions, but they still look impressive to dispassionate scrutineers. Behind his policies in both spheres, his distinctive statecraft can be discerned.

But there will always be debate about the issue which Sadat himself thought was at the heart of all historical problems: that of his influence over events. He saw himself, in all sincerity, as a maker of history — an executant of plans deeply laid and tenaciously pursued over a long period, a visionary who strove, and often succeeded, to make reality of his visions despite adverse circumstances. This image could be an honest delusion, made up of rationalisations after events which were really beyond his control, to which he merely responded in a series of brilliant and conspicuous but ultimately sterile extemporisations, *ad hoc* 'initiatives', gambles or calculated risks.

The truth probably lies between these extreme points of view. Sadat was genuinely a man of vision who sometimes, as we have seen, pulled off tremendous feats against all odds. But he tended to misrepresent some of his dextrous political footwork as a stately dance in which every step was planned in advance. Examples of the real influence of his vision on events are plentiful: the Egyptian-Israeli peace, the democratisation of Egyptian institutions, the liberalisation of the Egyptian economy, the realignment of Egyptian foreign policy, the forward planning for the colonisation of Egypt's deserts. Some of his inspirations were plucked, as it were, from a remote stratosphere of visionary planning: this was the sphere of his greatest successes. Others he seemed to find lying to hand in immediate problems and opportunities: on the whole, these were the starting-points of his less successful forays into the environmental and short-term economic fields.

This mixture of contrasting elements can be detected in the whole of his career. His political life unfolded — it seems, when one considers his capacity for planning — in a surprisingly unplanned, haphazard way, which is strangely intractable to analysis. His beginnings in politics are intelligible as part of a common pattern: birth into the ranks of a modest but politically important peasant élite — the 'second stratum' on whom all the régimes of recent Egyptian history have depended; education, dearly bought and resolutely pursued, adding urban experience to his rural origins and introducing him to the mental and social worlds of the real rulers of the nation; military service, drawing him into a milieu in which a revolutionary movement could take shape with him and to a great extent around him.

Sadat shared this sort of background with many other conspicuous figures — leaders and potential leaders — in recent Egyptian history. The causes for which he fought were common ones — Egyptian nationalism, anti-colonialism; the movements in which he worked — the Muslim Brotherhood and the Free Officers — were in the mainstream of Egypt's political development in the 'thirties and 'forties. But in those days, and for a long time afterwards, even though he was the effective founder of the Free Officers and an architect of the 1952 revolution, it was impossible to prophesy the greatness of Sadat's future role. He always skirted the centre of the stage, he always shunned the place of a leader. The roles he sought were important, but supportive and inconspicuous, out of the lime-light of worldly esteem — as spokesman, propagandist, writer, diplomatist, reconciler and parliamentary speaker. He had a great talent for power — acquiring it, handling it, exploiting it for the good — which, however, he forbore to deploy until the very greatest responsibilities were thrust upon him, and which astonished the world when it was revealed.

Once he became president, Sadat's life assumed an aspect of consistency and fixity of course absent from his early checkered career (when only fixity of purpose had been apparent). This was because he grasped the opportunity to devote himself to the unremitting pursuit of long-cherished objectives, which had never before seemed practicable: the elimination of dependency from Egypt's relations with foreign powers, especially the Soviet Union: the rectification — as he saw it — of the course of the revolution; the recovery of national spirit; the restoration of individual freedoms; the creation of Egyptian democracy; the struggle for prosperity; the achievement of peace. At home, the tenor of his policies may be described in part as modernist, liberal, pragmatic, and rationalist — a culmination of the western-influenced, but not western-dominated, secular Egyptian tradition of thought of the late nineteenth and twentieth centuries. But this would be a simplification, only partly right. Similarly, it is all too easy to see Sadat's work in terms of a reaction against the excesses of the Nasser years: the roots of the tradition in which Sadat stood go back much beyond the time of his predecessor. It is true that he corrected many of Nasser's mistakes, but he also sought to uphold what he interpreted as the kernel of his friend's work and goals — the things that formed their common heritage. He continued to oppose Marxism and clerical obscurantism alike. He continued to steer Egypt between the rival fanaticisms to which so many of her neighbours have fallen prey.

While consistent with recent Egyptian history, Sadat's policy was founded on a deep sense of continuity with a remoter past. At the same time as being modernist and pragmatic, Sadat's outlook was traditionalist and profoundly principled. We have seen in particular how his sense of history, his traditional nationalism, and his intense if undogmatic Islamic spirituality inspired and animated all he tried to do for Egypt. Part of the explanation for this can be found, as we have seen, in Sadat's background and the events of his life. The fact that it was a life so thoroughly representative of Egypt helps to account for the acceptability his policies won among the people. The extent of his shared outlook with fellow Egyptians was a product of all that he had in common with them. The same may be said of the keynotes of his foreign policy: independence and peace are goals which the entire Egyptian nation has long craved and for which generation after generation has made terrible sacrifices.

Of course, there were other sources of Sadat's success. His achievements were too personal to be explicable merely as parts of historical processes. Yet in exploring his personality, the identity for which his own autobiography represented his search, no observer has ever really made more than superficially successful forays. The strength Sadat's faith gave him contributed enormously to his powers. He evidently owed an immense amount to his family, especially to his wife. We have seen how Jihan's life complemented his own in an extraordinary way. Like him, an intellectual; like him, a modernist who has championed female emancipation; yet, like him, a traditionalist too, saturated in hand-me-down values; like him, an Egyptian fired in the kiln of the nationalist struggle from the clays of the Nile valley; yet, like him, a humane and tolerant seeker after peace. The high value Jihan placed on traditional wifely virtues, combined with the boldness with which she has been prepared to enter unconventional arenas in support of her husband or in pursuit of social goals, made her a useful helpmate. And the climate she created in the Sadat family and presidential 'rest-houses' made their calm, harmonious household a retreat and base from which the president could work in his characteristic, contemplative fashion.

Finally, Sadat was a master of the theatre of public life, a brilliant extemporiser of speeches and initiatives — which is not to say he was a mere opportunist: he usually exploited his chances in pursuit of long-term plans. He had the headline-capturing talent that is indispensable in modern politics. His knowledge of the world's media and of mass communication was uncanny. He was as spellbinding as he was prolific in giving interviews. If one area of Egypt's excessively cumbrous bureaucracy served him well, it was the state information services; on the other hand, it was he who provided them with the subject-matter for first rate copy. Egypt had many qualifications for a conspicuous world role, but Sadat's gift for international publicity riveted global attention in a peculiarly forceful way.

Today, after the years of endurance and achievement we have described, after the crisis of 1971 and the president's untimely death, Sadat is entering a long period of posthumous scrutiny of his reputation. All the successes we have reviewed in these pages are responsible for that reputation but will not necessarily guarantee it in perpetuity. Only durability for the peace he has brought to the Middle East, or success for Egypt in solving, in her own sphere, world economic problems, can ensure permanence for the esteem in which Sadat was once so widely held. At the moment, the prospects on both scores are problematical but on the whole auspicious. Though outstanding causes of conflict between Israel and her neighbours are likely to remain unresolved for some time, the momentum of peace is not altogether extinguished and should be resumed as some of the main countries and organisations involved pass through internal political changes.

Sadat laboured incessantly to broaden the peace process to include all the parties directly involved and to deploy the peacemaking talents of organisations on the sidelines, like the E.E.C. There is no discernible likelihood of an early recrudescence of war: re-alignment of the Arab camp is impossible until after Egypt recovers the last fragments of Sinai in 1982. And every moment of quiet, every new form of Israeli-Arab contact, every shift of opinion within Israel in favour of realism and of regional co-operation increases the chances of permanent peace. Already, what Sadat called the 'vicious circle of hate' is attenuated, if not finally broken.

On the economic front Egypt has apparently passed through the gruelling tests of the 'seventies. Economic growth exceeds 9% p.a. The country is enjoying record foreign exchange earnings. The world's biggest housing programme is an instance of how society is benefiting from the increase of wealth. And foreign confidence, manifest in record levels of investment in 1980, continued in 1981 until Sadat's death.

Though the world economic climate is capable only of very slow and erratic improvement in the 'eighties, Egypt should be better prepared to cope with the problems thanks to enhanced oil production and the increased exploitation of the natural resources of the desert. The distribution through social planning of the growing benefits of economic progress will help to anchor the stability of Egyptian politics and society. Egypt's new constitution enables Sadat's successor to look forward to a long presidency, sanctioned by plebiscite. It also commits Egypt to a democratic and Islamic course — guaranteeing two of Sadat's declared 'aspirations' for his country — by entrenching the mixed economy, declaring the Sharia to be the source of all law, guaranteeing the multi-party system and an independent press, and instituting a second chamber: in short, giving a framework of potential permanence to his work and embodying the 'state of institutions' he announced more than ten years ago, in a way that will exclude would-be pashas and sultans from power for as long as the constitution lasts. The biggest threat is from the forces of Islamic revolution.

Sadat has been branded as 'another Shah'. But in Egypt's confessionally variegated, cosmopolitan society an Islamic revolution on the Iranian pattern would make little sense. The overt despotism, the palpable exploitation, and the massive foreign presence which fomented discontent in Iran are not present in Egypt. The revolutionaries are numerous enough to be a constant source of anxiety but too few to realise their aims. The trend inaugurated by Sadat's reforms is more likely to lead to greater democracy than to alternative forms of tyranny. Egypt is working towards fulfilment of the promise Sadat made in an anniversary meditation on Nasser's death in September 1974:

> As I ponder on the greatest task I ought to devote myself to, after liberation of our land is completed, I can think of only one: to hand over this revolution to its owner, the people. The people is its own master, it possesses the right to determine its own future and to choose the way of life it likes. All we have to do is to afford it the freedom to make that choice [Israeli, 670].

The system will probably work better without Sadat. The nervous reactions to problems which marred his last year, the tendency to treat democracy as a child he could chasten at will, and the allure of autocracy, which had an increasing fascination for him as his difficulties multiplied, might have endangered his own work had he lived.

Above all, perhaps, Sadat's historical stature is guranteed by two qualities that shone through his statecraft. On the one hand, he showed tremendous historical resilience, an ability to take initiatives which transcend the force of circumstances and change the course of events. His politics were, as he said, 'the art of the impossible'. On the other hand, he always had the power to surprise, to perform some arresting *coup de théâtre* which enlivens the political process, quickens change, and leaves participants and observers gaping. The first of these qualities is a mark of real greatness, recalling Napoleon's apophthegm that greatness consists in the ability to master fortune. The second is more a quality of conspicuous brilliance, which made Sadat one of the best known (if still least thoroughly understood) of modern statesmen. Both qualities gave everything Sadat did in the political sphere a challenging freshness and originality. He created a new kind of practical political philosophy of the unexpected, by inverting staatspolitik and putting morality and integrity first.

For whatever becomes of Sadat's reputation and of Sadat's Egypt in future years, his claim to a commitment to pursue integrity is unlikely ever to be seriously impugned. Few leaders can make with utter sincerity the retrospective judgement he hazarded in his autobiography in 1978:

> Each step I have taken over the years has been for the good of
> Egypt, and has been designed to serve the cause of right,
> liberty and peace [Sadat, 1979 p. 1].

The clarity with which he pursued that cause can still be glimpsed, even through the haze of failure that gathered in the last months of his life. If, in the next generation, the cause of peace is advanced, economic co-operation in the Middle East achieved or brought nearer, the energy problems of Egypt solved or the population of Egypt more rationally distributed — if any of these things happens it will be in great part thanks to Sadat's vision and efforts. He died at a critical moment for his reputation. But in the long term his fame is likely to revive.

Egypt after Sadat

In the short term, much of Sadat's work is certain to be repudiated in his own country. In part, this is because of the historic oscillations of Egyptian opinion, which is dissatisfied with any characterisation of change as less than revolutionary. Nasser made a *tabula rasa* of the past. Sadat launched his own reaction against Nasserism with a 'Corrective Revolution'. The new president, resenting life in a giant's shadow as much as Sadat resented Nasser's, is anxious — as Sadat was in his time — to dissociate himself from aspects of his mentor's style and methods with which he disagrees. He is already making the same sort of deprecating gestures towards his predecessor's reputation as Sadat made in the early 'seventies towards that of Nasser. It is impossible to get President Mubarak even to say anything specifically about Sadat. When he feels he has established sufficient independence from Sadat's political legacy and achieved a clearly defined public image for himself, he will no doubt criticise his former master openly. Meanwhile, by dismantling the cult of personality with which Sadat sought to shore up his position in his last years of power, by discontinuing the wooing of the world's press, which made Sadat famous or notorious, and by symbolic gestures like the abolition, and even demolition, of presidential rest-houses, Mubarak has promised change by implication — change, at least, of style.

Amid these reversals of style and reputation, it is worth asking how much of Sadat's political legacy will survive. In particular, three crucial policies — crucial not only for Egypt but for the whole western world — hang in the balance. First, will the basis of Egyptian economic policy continue to be *infitah*? Secondly, will Egypt continue to espouse Middle East peace and, specifically, will Egypt continue to pursue peace along the lines laid down by Sadat at Camp David? Thirdly, will the development of Egyptian democracy continue to be modelled on western patterns? On the answers to these questions most of the unresolved problems about Egyptian policy after Sadat depend. By them Egypt's global alignment will be determined. The reasons for believing that Egypt's future policies in all these key respects will in effect be continuations of Sadat's work have been themes of the whole of this book. But the questions are important enough to warrant a final synoptic review.

The survival of *infitah* is likely on a 'Hobson's choice' basis. The policy has been assiduously maligned. But its supposed ill effects would probably have happened anyway and it is hard to see any viable alternative. Neither President Mubarak not any of his ministers has so far been willing, clearly or comprehensively, to repudiate *infitah.* Among the criticisms voiced against the policy, four main themes are discernible: *infitah* has brought about a form of neo-colonialism in which foreign investors dominate vital areas of the Egyptian economy; it discriminates against the poor; it has created a class of middlemen whose values and behaviour are offensive to most of the rest of society; and because of imperfections in the distribution of benefits, it has caused unrest and political instability. None of these criticisms is altogether sound. In the first place, the entire world today is bound together by bonds of economic interdependence. There can be no industrial or commercial *fará da se* — and Egypt is now inextricably committed to an industrial and commercial future. Her vast and growing population cannot be sustained by any other means. The exploitation of Egypt's resources by foreign investors hardly merits the name 'neo-colonialism' as long as it is subject to Egyptian political control. The problem of political control evaded or over-trumped by multinational business giants is not confined to Egypt or even to the developing world. To curtail foreign investment as a means of curbing the multi-nationals would be an oblique and self-damaging overreaction. The Egyptian government continues to dominate economic life in the country by the sheer weight of the capital it commands, the manpower it musters, and the market-share it wields. The greatest obstacle to economic progress, indeed, comes arguably from the inhibitions and inefficiencies of an excessively corpulent public sector, while the dynamic private sector would be cripplingly undercapitalised without foreign help.

An aspect of *infatah* which more plausibly conforms to a 'neo-colonialist' model is the relatively high share of U.S. government aid among the sources of foreign capital. This has largely been confined to public-sector enterprises, but its scale has left Egypt in a position of reliance on the Americans ominously reminiscent of the dependence on the Soviet Union from which Sadat had to extricate his country in his early years of power. This problem has been or has become real enough in the last three years. But so far it has had few political effects: it has been a result of Egypt's political re-alignments, not their cause. It has not impeded Egypt from independent decision-making. American tutelage always tends to be loosely felt compared with that of Russia, and Egypt is too important a country ever to be left without room for manœuvre. The over-emphasis of American aid has been an essentially temporary phenomenon. As sources of aid multiply, as Egypt's many suitors return, inevitably, to woo her, the problem will be less acutely felt and will virtually solve itself. No dramatic policy-change at the top is needed.

Nor are the alleged social ills of *infitah* really such as they have been represented. Though it is true that Sadat failed to communicate with the poor, his policies were not to their disadvantage. And while the middleman class in Egypt has grown enormously in the last generation, *infitah* has contributed to the phenomenon rather than caused it. The mood of *enrichissez-vous* needed little government encouragement to generate action once the opportunities for accumulating wealth developed naturally in the late 'sixties and early 'seventies as a result of Egypt's close relations with the developing world and especially with the Arabs. Arab oil and the chances of employment abroad at lucrative salaries which took Egyptians away from home in their hundreds of thousands created many a nexus of wealth-creation and consumption back home through the remittances of expatriates. Today, two million Egyptians — to judge from official statistics, though estimates by independent researchers suggest the figure may be slightly lower — work abroad, most of them in the Arab world, despite discrimination against Egyptians after Camp David. With their dependants they constitute a huge minority in Egypt — about ten million people, living on the fruits of high income, with spending-power enormously greater than that of their fellow countrymen who have no skills worth selling abroad. To abandon *infitah* in order to eliminate invidious inequalities from Egypt would be folly against this background.

Of course there remains a strictly economic case against *infitah.* The successes of the policy have not matched expectations. Investment was slow to rise after 1974. Even the progress made towards peace in 1977 brought the levels of foreign investment to no more than $300 m. above normal levels. Much of the investment that has been forthcoming has gone into unproductive developments — tourism, for instance, and prestige projects. These are fair points. But *infitah* has to be judged against the available alternatives, not the wildly over-optimistic expectations with which it was launched, when Sadat, suffering from an excess of optimism acute even by his standards, hoped for an additional $15-20 billion of investment within a few years [Hamed, 1981, 8]. Economic liberalisation may not have worked the wonders asked of it, but it is the only means to progress Egypt has. The origins of *infitah,* indeed, go back to the slow dawning of realisation of this fact in Nasser's last years, when, for instance, the 30th March Political and Economic Programme of 1968 inaugurated the first moves towards economic liberalisation. The conditions that made Nasser take the first faltering steps in this direction are present still. The policy preceded Sadat in one form and will survive him in one form or another.

As for the question whether Egypt under Mubarak will continue to follow the path pointed from Camp David, any answer must care-fully distinguish reality from rhetoric. A verbal disavowal of Camp David seems certain once Israeli withdrawal from Sinai is completed — more or less simultaneously with the appearance of this book. No way forward in the peace process is possible without such a disavowal, because too many parties have invested too much prestige in denouncing Sadat's approach to peace. So many people believe that Camp David damaged Sadat's régime that, like most lies, it has devel-oped a momentum of its own. Falsehoods men believe are always more powerful than the truths they deny. In the realm of rhetoric, there-fore, Camp David will have to be abandoned if the reality of peace is to be saved. Yet the peace that will prevail in the Middle East in years to come will continue to owe everything to Camp David. Although deterrence in the region has reached a point where no party dares start a major war, or, if there is a recrudescence of conflict, it will be vicarious — in the Lebanon, for instance, or conceivably in the Sudan, or between Arabs — or limited and brief.

The future of Egyptian democracy will also remain indebted to Sadat's glutinous legacy. Ironically, Sadat himself curtailed democracy in his last year of life by his over-sensitivity to criticism. Freedom of the press was limited. New political activity was discouraged. President Mubarak's task is to recover the momentum Sadat set at an earlier stage of his presidency. A western-style multi-party format is bound to remain the Egyptian model, even though it has a poor track record. Before the 1952 Revolution, party democracy failed because the parties were mere factions representing, for the most part, a small political nation. Since Sadat's reintroduction of parties the party system has had little chance to show what it can achieve, because the president's own parties so dominated elections that political pluralism was more effective in theory than in practice. Yet Sadat did enough to determine an irreversible trend. Constitutionalism, political rights, a free press, free universities and the framework of a party system are too highly prized in Egypt today to be easily discarded. A return to Nasserist paternalism, in which political rights were sacrificed for the sake of meagre economic gains, is unthinkable. The alternative models to that of the western world — Islamic revolution in its versions by Gaddafy or Khomeini — is unpalatable to most Egyptians, with their long traditions of contact with the west. The nature of the parties will have to change. Sadat conjured them out of the Arab Socialist Union and his own conception of what the country needed. In future, to work really successfully, the parties will have to come, like Egypt's saints' cults, from popular energies and popular demands. But this will be a modification within the Sadat tradition, not a new departure.

Finally, in this connection, the cult of personality for which Sadat was so deeply criticised, the paternalistic posture he adopted towards his people, are bound to re-emerge in Egypt, even though President Mubarak has concentrated his reaction against Sadat's style of presidency on these things. Abject devotion to the head of state is deeply imbedded in Egyptian popular culture. It comes through in numerous proverbs which venerate authority and confuse public authority with the person of the head of state. Absolutism seems natural to the peasants who form the greater part of Egypt's masses.

Peasant respondents to the questions posed by Atif Fuad, a researcher from Cairo's Ain Shams University, were unquestioning in their attitude to the President as father of his people. '*Rais* is all in all', said one. 'He has the right to do whatever he wishes. It's our duty to obey *Rais* and depend on Allah and on him.' Another respondent made his personal understanding of the nature of political authority equally clear. 'As long as Sadat exists, it does not make a difference whether we have or have not legislatures, political parties and local councils' [El-Menoufi, 1982, 86-87]. Although President Mubarak's present image is emphatically uncharismatic — as Sadat's was when he first came to the job — he will soon start reflecting the in-built charisma of the system. He may be disinclined to engineer, to orchestrate his public cult, as Sadat did, but he will be unable to escape his destiny as the peasants' pharaoh. From the perspective of a few years hence, the history of all Egypt's post-revolutionary presidencies will probably look remarkably continuous in this respect.

On a broader level, beyond these pressing problems of immediate interest, Egypt has now to confront the great historic dilemmas that Sadat left unresolved. For at least a hundred years, since the abortive revolution of Ahmad Urabi, Egyptian intellectuals have been engaged in an impassioned search for a collective identity for the Egyptian people — a search in which Sadat shared and to which he alluded in the title of his autobiography. At times during his career Sadat thought he had got to the end of the search: he toyed with an invented Egyptian ideology that was a mere intellectual construct, with no roots in what Egypt was really like. He then abandoned ideology altogether, dismissing it as chimerical, and concentrated on enhancing the historic character of the Egyptian community, making brilliant use of his appeals to village values and pharaonic echoes. But the real end of the quest escaped him as it has escaped his fellow searchers, perhaps because there is no end.

National character — if it exists at all — is mutable. As Sadat rightly saw, it is a product of history, but it can only be given an open-ended definition. It changes as the structure of a political nation changes, and as the members of the nation transform their own perceptions of their interests and their heritage and their enemies and their origins and all that enables them to identify with each other.

Identity crisis, perhaps, is essential to Egypt. Without it Egyptians would hardly be recognisable as Egyptians. Their dilemma began or became acute a hundred years ago because of the strains of the conjunction of divergent worlds — European and oriental, Christian and Islamic, agrarian and industrial, liberal and authoritarian, secular and religious — to which Egypt was a half-willing host at that time. Since then, Egyptians have hovered or lurched between rival visions of their country's future. Today, the dilemmas have hardened dangerously to a central core and concern above all else the question of the degree to which Egyptian identity will henceforth be distinctly Islamic. Sadat believed that Islam could be reconciled with the selective reception of western culture and science. He died, in a sense, a martyr to that belief. He was representative in that respect of the mainstream of Egyptian thought for at least a century — perhaps since the French invasion of 1798. But now there are increasing numbers of Egyptians who believe the two strands are incompatible and that the warp and weft of the fabric of modern Egyptian culture are about to fall apart. It is inescapably true that, while Islam is represented by revolutionary fanatics, no compromise devised by the technocrats and bourgeois professionals who still form the ruling élite will satisfy them. When one walks through the commercial streets of Cairo, with their rational layout, cosmopolitan crowds, multi-coloured shop-fronts sporting the names of owners from a rich diversity of historic and ethnic communities, and mingled mosques and churches reflective of the coexistence of every kind of religious persuasion, it seems incredible that this dazzling balance could ever be threatened by Islamic fanaticism. But the call of a muezzin on a downtown breeze and a violent daubing on a wall come as reminders that Egypt has a fundamental choice to make. There is no doubt that the new régime in Egypt will stand squarely in Sadat's tradition — and the tradition of all modern Egyptian governments — in confronting that choice.

Selected Further Reading
in European languages

M. Aulas, ed., *L'Égypte d'aujourd'hui* (Paris, 1977)

R.W. Baker, *Egypt's Uncertain Revolution under Nasser and Sadat* (Cambridge, Mass., 1978)

H. Barkai, 'Egypt's Economic Constraints', *Jerusalem Quarterly*, no. 14 (1980), 122-44

L. Binder, *In a Moment of Enthusiasm* (Chicago, 1978)

J.S. Birks and C.A. Sinclair, 'Egypt: a Frustrated Labour Exporter?', *Middle East Journal*, xxxiii (1979), 188-303

D.S. Brown, 'Egypt and the United States: Collaborators in Economic Development', *Middle East Journal*, xxxv (1981), 15-24

R.M. Burrell and A.R. Kelidar, *Egypt: the Dilemmas of a Nation, 1970-77* (Washington Papers, no. 48, Beverley Hills and London, 1977)

D.W. Carr, *Foreign Investment and Development in Egypt* (New York, 1979)

M.N. Cooper, 'Egyptian State Capitalism in Crisis: Economic Policies and Political Interests, 1967-71', *International Journal of Middle East Studies*, x (1979), 481-516

——, *The Transformation of Egypt* (London and Canberra, 1982)

Halim El-Dabh, 'The State of the Arts in Egypt Today', *Middle East Journal*, xxxiv (1981), 15-24

in

A.L. Dawisha, *Egypt in the Arab World* (London 1976)

Egypt in the New Middle East: MERIP Reports, no. 107 (July-August 1982)

P. Eidelberg, *Sadat's Strategy* (Dollard des Ormeaux, 1979)

Encyclopaedia Britannica Yearbook (Chicago, 1981)

H. Fawzi, 'Continuity of Egyptian Personality', *Jerusalem Quarterly*, no. 14 (1980), 3-7

D. Frescobaldi, *La sfida di Sadat* (Milan 1977)

M. Boutros Ghali, 'The Egyptian National Consciousness', *Middle East Journal*, xxii (1978), 59-77

A.L. Gray, Jr., 'Egypt's Ten Years' Economic Plan 1973-82', *Middle East Journal*, xxx (1976), 36-48

O. Hamed, 'Egypt's Open Door Economic Policy: an Attempt at Economic Integration in the Middle East', *International Journal of Middle East Studies*, xii (1981), 1-9

I. Harik, *The Political Mobilisation of Peasants: a Study of an Egyptian Community* (Bloomington, 1974)

M.H. Heikal, *The Road to Ramadan* (New York, 1975)

The Assassination of Sadat (forthcoming, 1983)

A.E. Hillal Dessouki, 'The Shift in Egypt's Migration Policy: 1952-78', *Middle Eastern Studies*, xviii (1982), 53-68

R.A. Hinnebusch, 'The National Progressive Unionist Party: the National-left Opposition in post-Populist Egypt', *Arab Studies Quarterly*, iii (1981), 325-51

D. Hirst and I. Beeson, *Sadat* (London, 1981)

D. Hopwood, *Egypt: Politics and Society 1945-81* (London 1982)

Saad Eddin Ibrahim, 'Anatomy of Egypt's Militant Islamic Groups', *International Journal of Middle East Studies,* xii (1980), 423-53

      -      , 'Egypt's Islamic Militants', *MERIP Reports,* no. 103 (February 1982), 5-14

R. Israeli, ed., *The Public Diary of President Sadat* (3 vols, Leiden, 1978-79)

E. Kanovsky, *The Egyptian Economy since the Mid-sixties: the Micro-sectors* (Tel-Aviv, 1978)

R. Mabro, *The Egyptian Economy* (Oxford, 1974)

K. El-Menoufi, 'The Orientation of Egyptian Peasants towards Political Authority between Continuity and Change', *Middle Eastern Studies,* xviii (1982), 82-93

K.R. Müller and M.W. Blaisse, *Anwar Sadat: the Last Hundred Days* (London, 1981)

D.M. Reid, 'Return of the Egyptian Wafd', *International Journal of African Historical Studies,* xii (1979)

Revue de la presse égyptienne (Aix-en-Provence, 1981 -)

A.Z. Rubinstein, *Red Star over the Nile* (Princeton, 1977)

Sadat: Man of Peace (London, 1979)

Anwar El-Sadat, *Révolte sur le Nil* (Paris, 1957): *Revolt on the Nile* (London, 1957); page references in the text of the present book are to the English edition

      -      , *President Anwar El-Sadat's Policies* (Cairo, 1971)

      -      , 'Where Egypt Stands', *Foreign Affairs* (October, 1972)

      -      , *In Search of Identity* (New York, 1977; London 1978)

N. Salem-Babikian, 'The Sacred and the Profane: Sadat's Speech to the *Knesset',* *Middle East Journal,* xxxiv (1980), 13-24

F.M. Shalaby, *Der Wandel der ägyptischen Aussenpolitik unter Sadat, 1970 bis 1977* (Bonn, 1979)

G. Shoukri, *Égypte: contre-révolution* (Paris, 1979)

E.N. Slaieh, 'The October War and Sadat's Year of Decision', *International Political Science Review,* x, no. 2 (1976)

R. Springborg, 'Patrimonialism and Policy-making in Egypt: Nasser and Sadat and the Tenure Policy for Reclaimed Lands', *Middle Eastern Studies,* xv (1979), 49-69

M.W. Suleiman, 'Changing Attitudes towards Women in Egypt: the Role of Fiction in Women's Magazines', *Middle Eastern Studies,* xiv (1978), 352-71

P.J. Vatikiotis, *Nasser and his Generation* (London, 1978)

J. Waterbury, 'Egypt: the wages of Dependency' in A.L. Udovitch, ed., *The Middle East: Oil, Conflict and Hope* (Lexington, 1976)

      -      , *Egypt: Burdens of the Past, Options for the Future* (Bloomington, 1978)

A. Winkel, *Jehan el Sadat: First Lady und Frauenrechtlerin am Nil* (Koblenz, 1976)

B. Witte, 'Fünf Jahre Sadat', *Europa-Archiv,* xxx (1975)

Index